MW00881282

GEORGE
BARNU

01144

789 4

779 173

339757

48 33

Tools For Tomorrow

Memoirs of Paul E. Pentz

PAUL E. PENTZ

authorHOUSE®

AuthorHouse™
1663 Liberty Drive
Bloomington, IN 47403
www.authorhouse.com
Phone: 1-800-839-8640

First published by AuthorHouse 8/19/2009

ISBN: 978-1-4490-1682-1 (sc)

Printed in the United States of America
Bloomington, Indiana

This book is printed on acid-free paper.

Forward

While Carolyn and I were having dinner with friends Fritz and Kathy Friday one evening we talked about our younger days when we went as families to fishing camps. We reminisced about cooking on wood stoves and heating the cabin with pot belly wood stoves and using out houses. Somehow the conversation got around to how sad it is that our grandchildren will never be exposed to "roughing it" as we had so much enjoyed. Someone said those long lost memories should be recorded so that our grandchildren would have some understanding from whence we came.

I awoke that night about one o'clock with my head spinning with thoughts of experiences that I would love to communicate to our family. Returning to sleep was out of the question so I went into the office and started typing.

We see our children and grandchildren too infrequently because of the different geographic areas in which we live. When we are together it seems that conversations focus on what's for dinner or to what restaurant do we want to go or what is planned for tomorrow's activities. Rarely do we spend time talking about family history or what has brought us to our present environment. It seems as though life goes too fast today for anyone to take the time to look back and reminisce.

This book was written partially as a brief family history and partially to share some of the lessons that I have learned and some of the values that have been important to my success. It is my hope that our children will be amused and that our grandchildren might learn from the lessons that are noted here.

CHAPTER I

The Beginning

On February 16, 1940 I arrived into this world at a hospital in Rockville Center, New York. Our family actually lived on Bayview Avenue in Freeport, New York. That is what people would say was out on the Island, Long Island.

I had one older brother, Bob, who they nicknamed Pen so as not to be confused with his father who was also Bob. In the tradition of men in those days the first son was usually named after the father. This then became the namesake and the apple of the father's eye, no different in our family. That type of closeness is natural because from the earliest of years the eldest son is more ready to join the father in fishing or claming or other activities which were popular in that area at that time.

Dad was born in Astoria, New York, his father being an iron worker and his mother taking whatever jobs she could to help put food on the table. Grandpa Pentz had run away from home when he was a small child and never went back. He came from Maine and somehow ended up in New York but I never knew how. He had no schooling and therefore was illiterate and couldn't even sign his own name, he used an X. He was very embarrassed about this and did everything he could to hide it from everyone. In spite of or perhaps because of his handicap he became an iron worker, walking the high beams on construction sites like the Chrysler Building, The Empire State Building, and the Brooklyn Bridge.

Iron workers were paid well because of the great risk they took. Grandpa had an unusual habit though, he liked to travel. Grandma used to have to hide as much money as she could because when Grandpa had a pocketful he was inclined to hop a freight train and disappear for unknown periods of time. When he ran out of money he would reappear and go back to work.

Grandma was half Shinecock Indian and half something else. She was less than five feet tall but a powerhouse of intelligence, energy, courage, and fun. She literally held the family together putting up with the idiosyncrasies of her husband. She used to say that fights were tough but making up was really fun. That was born out by the fact that they brought five children into this world. Unfortunately two died shortly after childbirth (they didn't go to the hospital to have children in those days, they had a midwife come in) and Dad's older brother drowned while swimming with him under the Hellgate Bridge in New York. Dad was eight at the time and his brother Clarence was twelve.

Dad had a younger sister Dorothy, "Dot", who contracted polio in her early years and was diagnosed to never be able to walk. As testimony to the strength of Grandma Pentz, she refused to accept that and daily massaged Dot's legs for hours increasing the circulation and gradually bringing life back into those dead limbs. She was successful and Aunt Dot in her teens won many dance contests.

Mom was born in Carthage, New York way up above Syracuse and Buffalo in the cold country. Her mother and father were both teachers. One could teach in those days with only a high school education because few people went on the college. However, Grandpa Meeker, Clarence, went on to college and graduated from Albany Law School which was a rare accomplishment in 1907.

Grandpa was appointed Secretary of Labor for the State of New York under the Republican administration and later left that position when the Democrats took control of the state. He tried criminal law and was successful in winning his first case only to have the client thank him and tell him he was actually guilty. This was so devastating to a man of his ethics that he quit criminal law and went into real estate law. They moved to St. Albans, New York, a suburb of New York City. Grandpa commuted by train to New York and never drove a car in his life.

Grandma Meeker was extremely bright and well educated. We used to joke that she was so smart she did the New York Times crossword puzzles in ink. Her career was as a housewife raising my mother Josephine and her older sister Louise. She had a great sense of humor and I fondly remember her chuckle to Grandpa's ho ho ho.

With the frugal money management of Grandma Pentz, and the good earnings of Grandpa Pentz their family also moved to St. Albans and lived around the corner from the Meekers. That is how Mom and Dad met, on a bus going into the city.

The here again, gone again, tendencies of Grandpa Pentz often didn't put enough money in the kitty to take care of the family so Dad had to quit school when he was thirteen and go to work in New York for International Paper Company as an office boy. Determined to get his education he went to the school and asked if he could take the books home and read them and eventually take the tests which afforded him a high school diploma. I think Mon helped him with his schoolwork as their love blossomed. He was a quick study in everything except mechanical things.

With that background, it is safe to say that Dad was the most competitive person I ever met. He was determined to be the best at everything, to win whatever sporting event he was in, to catch the largest fish, and to earn the most money, and to get the next promotion.

Mom inherited the brilliance of her parents. Unfortunately she was unable to go to college as her parents only had enough money to send Louise to college. I guess that is just as well or I likely would never have come along. She worked as a secretary for Metropolitan Life Insurance in New York City. When they married Dad paid the newspaper not to put the wedding announcement in the paper because if metropolitan found out she was married they would have fired her. This was depression time, 1933, and married women were not allowed to work. One job per family and that only if you were lucky.

Once she became pregnant with my brother she had to quit and did not return to the workforce.

CHAPTER II

Dad's Early Career

At some time Oneida Paper Products which was a printed flexible packaging company was spun off from International Paper Company to the ownership of three men, Adolph Zucker, Sam Stein, and Gerald Fox. Dad went along with the package.

Sometime early on in the depression Dad was laid off. Having been a successful prize fighter he decided the only way he could earn money was to turn professional boxer. Fortunately he was brought back to work before his first professional fight or he probably would have gotten his butt handed to him. He had been quite successful as an amateur as I have a gold watch that he won in one of the first ever broadcast fights on New York radio.

These were the days of prohibition when alcoholic beverages were not allowed in this country. Alcohol was allowed in Canada and the porters on the trains running between Canada and New York bootlegged alcohol into the city. As office boy he was asked to take charge of managing the illicit liquor supply for the company as go between to pick up the orders from the friendly porter. I'm sure this liquor supply was used for entertainment functions and to stock the home liquor cabinets of the owners.

Since Dad was giving the porter a lot of business he would occasionally tip Dad with a free bottle or two. As Dad did not drink in those days he sold what he received to save money so that he could marry Mom.

Another way that Dad made money was by playing pool at lunch hour at the local pool hall. Apparently he was pretty good. On his first effort he won a silver dollar which he gave to Mom and said this is the first dollar we will save for our marriage. She still has that silver dollar today and used to wear it in a necklace.

On a fortunate day when everyone was out to lunch except Dad there was a telephone call from someone they had been trying to sell to with no previous luck. Somehow with his gift of gab Dad took an order much to the surprise of the owners. Mr. Fox was Vice President of Sales and he said I think you could learn to be a salesman and promoted him. At one point he expressed that Dad seemed to be a natural and wondered what he could do to further his career. Dad said let me sit in your office one day each week and just listen to how you run the business. That was the beginning of a great career.

Chapter III

Freeport, New York 1940 – 1944

Of course I was too young to actually remember what went on in those early years but I can recite some of the things I have been told. We lived on Bay View Avenue in a small house. My mother, Father, brother Pen, (four years older) and our Cocker Spaniel, Buffy who was bought for Pen at age two, made up the family.

These were war years with Japan bombing Pearl Harbor on December 7, 1941. Like all men Dad went to the draft but was rejected due to a broken ear drum and the fact that he could not see out of his left eye. A broken ear drum was automatic rejection because in a gas attack the gas would get in through your ear and no gas mask could protect you. He spent the war as an air raid warden.

I vaguely remember the blackouts when the sirens would go off and all lights had to go out and Dad would put on his helmet and man whatever post he was assigned to. We never actually had an attack from the air but I guess there were some torpedoes that sank some ships just off of our coast.

Everyone was encouraged to have a victory garden because food was directed overseas to support the troops and there was not enough left for those at home. We had a large vegetable garden and Dad built a chicken coop where he housed 100 chickens for eggs and chicken dinner.

There was no gas for the car so it had to be put up on blocks in the garage for storage until fuel could be purchased.

Chickens require feed and chicken feed attracts rats. On weekend mornings Pen would watch out the window and occasionally see a rat in the yard and wake Dad to inform him. He would slide up the bedroom window, stick out his double barrel twelve gauge shotgun and let loose. He would quickly close the window and go back to bed while the police patrolled the neighborhood to see where the shooting had come from. They never found out.

Another amusing trick he had was when he slaughtered a chicken. Southerners like Carolyn's grandmother simply wrung their necks but anyone that has chopped the head off a chicken knows that they run around without a head for some time. Dad couldn't take this. He would tie the chicken's feet to a small sapling, bend it toward the chopping block, chop the head off and let the sapling loose so that the chicken would flap hanging from the tree rather than running blindly and would bleed out.

In an effort to keep the chicken feed from the rats he put it inside the car standing on blocks in the garage.

This was a mistake. At least one smart rat found a way partially into the car but got stuck and died. Dad took the stinky car to the service station and told them to wash it and "Oh, by the way a squirrel seems to have gotten caught up in the car and would they get it out". When he picked up the car the attendant said "Squirrel my ass".

Mom tells me that when I was about two they had given me a penny to play with. It disappeared and for some reason they panicked and thought I had swallowed it. They took me to the doctor for either an x-ray or fluoroscope and could find nothing. Finally they asked me what happened to the penny and I reached into my pocket and pulled it out.

When I was a little guy I had a little girl friend, Judy Nelson who lived two doors away. One day when I was perhaps three I had gone down to play with her and she was taking a nap. Mom became alarmed that she could not find me and got everyone out looking for me. The Nelsons had a walled front porch and they eventually found me asleep sitting on their milk box on the front porch waiting for Judy to wake up.

In those days bottled (quart glass bottles) milk was delivered to the door about every other day and put in milk boxes on the front stoop. The milk man would also put some ice in the box to preserve the milk. There was no such thing as homogenized milk so each bottle was white milk on the bottom and heavy cream that had risen to the top. When you wanted a drink the milk had to be shaken to mix the cream with the milk. Also at that time refrigeration was just becoming popular transitioning from the ice boxes. I recall even years later seeing the ice man go up my Grandmother's street with his wagonload of ice and his tongs and leather shoulder protector to deliver to the homes that did not yet have electric refrigeration.

In early 1945 Dad was promoted to plant manager for Oneida's production facility in Baltimore so we moved.. He was responsible for production and sales which was quite a jump for him. We moved from Freeport to Baltimore and lived on Gibbons Avenue in what I recall as duplexes or common wall housing.

CHAPTER IV

Baltimore, Maryland 1945

We were only in Baltimore for one year and even though I was small my favorite memory was watching the men steam crabs in beer and spices. I have reinforced that fond memory many times since.

I recall going to the meat market with Dad when he would take a bottle of booze in a brown bag to bribe the butcher. Meat was rationed but this seemed to be enough to loosen the restrictions. We ate well.

Actually, we were there on both VE Day and VJ Day. I remember my brother and me standing on the corner beating pots and pans cheering for the national victory. I didn't really know the significance of what I was doing but joined the rest cheerfully.

Dad apparently made a little money then and became too strongly enamored with the game of golf. He left early in the morning and stayed out most of the day every Saturday and Sunday. One Saturday after he left, Mom took Pen and me on the train to Washington to the Zoo. We stayed all day or at least long enough to drive Dad crazy with fear upon finding the house empty. Mom called him and asked do you want me to come home or to take the kids and go home to my parents? If you want me to come home there will be no more golf on Sundays. She won easily and Dad never played golf again on Sunday until we kids were grown and both of them could play together. Mom was quietly strong.

Those were the days when washing machines had crank ringers instead of spinners. At that time automatic rollers were invented which were dangerous. I recall the boy down the street getting his arm caught in one and having it broken in several places.

I learned to ride a bicycle in Baltimore. There was no such thing as training wheels so Dad would run along side until I had my balance. Fortunately I had good balance. Unfortunately the day after I learned to ride a bike I was holding out one of those artificial birds on a stick that sing louder the faster you go. I was so impressed with the bird that I forgot to watch where I was going and ran into a parked car and broke a rib.

Enough of Baltimore.

CHAPTER V

Los Angeles, California 1946

Dad was promoted quickly again to run the west coast operation. We moved to a rental home in Los Angeles at 2328 Griffith Park Boulevard where we lived for a year until they found a home for us. Mom of course was reluctant to move that far from her family so some type of concession was made that provided for her to take Pen and me to New York every other year.

The trip to California was interesting. We took the Super Chief train, the best at the time, and had our own drawing room. It had a small bathroom, bunk beds for Pen and me and some other bed for Mom and Dad. With the four of us and a dog it was a bit crowded but we made do. Buffy, our dog was with us so any time the train stopped Dad had to quickly take her out. She was very particular and would not go unless she could do it on grass. Dad had to race our of the stations and look for grass. In those days no one thought about pooper scoopers or picking up after dogs, so we left a trail of deposits across the country. We were always worried that Dad wouldn't get back to the train in time but he did.

I recall Mom staying up all night when the train climbed the Rockies. She said it chugged slowly all the way at a very slow pace. We also watched out the window as Indians tried to sell beads to passengers when we stopped in Needles, California. It was 10:00 PM and it was still 110 degrees. Needles is frequently the hottest city in the U.S.

Across the street from our home on the other side of a field there was a small Italian grocery store/deli. The owner was helped by his daughter who was probably in her thirties. She took a shine to me and I would frequently go over there and she would fix me lunch to have with her in the backroom. Once she took me to some fancy restaurant and had our picture taken together.

At six years old I made friends with a boy my age Roger Burgess who lived well up the hill behind us. There was a vacant lot next to Roger's house and he and I dug a little fort in the middle of it. One day we were playing with matches, a strict no-no, and caught the field on fire. Terrified, I ran home thinking I would be caught and sent to jail. Fortunately, Roger's older brother realized what had happened and ran into the field to retrieve the evidentiary matches before the firemen got there. I hid in the corner of my room but Mom with her sharp nose smelled the smoke on me. No one was hurt, and no serious damage was done but we did get a severe scolding.

One day when our parents were up playing bridge with the Burgesses, Pen and I went home to get something. We walked in on a burglar. We quickly ran out and up the hill to get Dad. We went back with him and he loaded his double barrel twelve gauge shotgun. We went through the whole house and he would stand at the ready in front of each closet door and say Pen open the door. God help the poor burglar if he was still there. The next door neighbor told us she saw a man run out the back of our house and up the hill.

Chapter VI

Glendale, California 1946 – 47

Mom and Dad bought a nice little home at 1413 Sycamore Terrace in Glendale. It was on a hillside with tall palms lining each side of the road. During our first year there Mom, Pen and I flew back to New York for a month long visit. We had a two engine prop driven plane, I think a DC3 which didn't fly very high and must have caught every air pocket possible. The plane went up and down mercilessly. Everyone, including some sailors behind us was airsick. Everyone except Pen, he had an iron stomach. I believe the flight including several refueling stops was about a 23 hour trip. The return trip was on a four engine prop plane and was a bit less bumpy until we went over the Rockies. Sick again.

I was generally a quiet and polite little kid but I couldn't refuse a dare. During the heat of the days the tar on the street melted and I had collected a large ball of tar. One of the kids put the "double dog dare" on me to see if I could hit a moving car. I did with a big thud. The car screeched to a halt and we all ran. Near the road was some type of a tree whose branches hung down very thickly to the ground but provided a hollow inside. I ducked in there scared to death and hid while I heard the man look all around without finding me. When I heard the car drive off I ran home proud that I had survived the dare.

This was of course before television. I recall sitting outside in the driveway with Dad one Saturday afternoon listening to Joe Louis win one of his championship fights Dad having been a prize fighter was always interested in the fights and insisted that Pen and I learn to box. He bought us boxing gloves, gave us a few lessons and then would have us box with each other. With him eleven and me seven it wasn't much of a match. About two shots the face and I would have a nose bleed and be crying. I never really saw the fun in that lesson.

Men were back home from the war now and the roads were often thick with hitchhikers. Trusting people frequently gave them a lift. The man across the street picked up a hitchhiker who clubbed him over the head and robbed him. The beating left him mentally disturbed for life. That prompted our first lectures on the dangers of hitchhikers and strangers.

Pen had taken up the cello either in Los Angeles or in Glendale. He was a natural talent. He progressed rapidly and was soon involved in the Merimbloom Orchestra, a large and highly reputed orchestra. Every Saturday Mom, Pen, and I would take two busses and a trolley to get to their practice place. By the time we returned it took the entire day. He was auditioned by MGM for a movie but lost out to a smaller kid who also played the cello. He did play with the orchestra at the famed Shrine Auditorium which was quite an honor.

I recall Pen and me playing with sparklers one evening which was fine with our parents as long as we were careful and did not throw them. Of course it was neat to light a sparkler and throw it up in the night sky like a rocket. Being a block away from home and out of sight we were throwing them when one landed in the top of a large fir tree beside a house. We held our breaths waiting to see if the tree and the house would catch fire. Fortunately the sparkler burned out without catching the tree on fire. That ended our sparkler throwing.

CHAPTER VII

Ridgewood, New Jersey 1948 –1958

In 1948 Dad was promoted to National Sales Manager and we moved back to the east coast. We stayed a month or two with Mom's folks in St. Albans while we looked for a home. With both sets of grandparents living near each other we spent most days at Dad's folk's home playing cards and other games. As years went by the level of conversation at the homes of both sets of grandparents became more interesting at the Meeker's home and less interesting at the Pentz home. Obviously it was an education issue. Our time on visits shifted toward the Meeker's home.

Dad had researched communities and was determined to buy a home in Ridgewood, New Jersey, a very affluent and beautiful community. We spent a lengthy day with a realtor who kept showing us homes in the surrounding towns. It finally occurred to Dad that race was a problem. Dad worked for a company that was almost totally Jewish and he had a large flattened nose from boxing so his actions and appearance would make anyone think he was Jewish. I recall him saying to the realtor, "look I am not Jewish and if necessary I can prove it so let's stop fooling around and get into Ridgewood". We did, and bought a brand new house that day in Upper Ridgewood, the newer but nicer part of the town. The house seemed like a castle to us but it really was only three bedrooms and not very large.

Our home at 398 Hamilton Road (Dad said that was a Jewish street number because it was like a bargain price) was on a nice lot with all of the properties around us well manicured. It was a heavily wooded area with large oak trees everywhere and large tracts of forestland starting at the end of the street and going for considerable distances. There were large ponds and a good stream in the woodlands providing for good camping and fishing for us young boys. It was a very safe town so there was no concern about letting us boys spend great amounts of time anywhere we wanted to go.

Ridgewood was a high end bedroom community for executives who commuted to New York City or other places to work. The downtown area was filled with high class shops offering great services giving me my first taste of the good life. I liked it.

I lived in Ridgewood through high school and my folks continued on there until several years after Dad retired which was in 1974.

In my high school years, having learned a little bit about segregation, I looked back and wondered why the community would prevent Jews from moving in while they had a small Negro community. In those days no one heard of the term black in referencing a person. I never did figure that out.

Pen, now 12, applied for the Ridgewood Symphony Orchestra and became the first child to be accepted into that orchestra. He played first cello for them. There was a large newspaper article about him as if he were a child prodigy which perhaps he was.

We had a beautiful knotty pine basement with a bar and a ping pong table and tiled floor. It was great for our friends to come over to play. Pen always had an interest in guns and somehow bought a 22 rifle with a scope and a bullet trap. A bullet trap was a heavy steel device with angled walls that made the bullet ricochet so much that it ground itself into powder by the time it reached the cylindrical catching device at the end. In sighting the scope he forgot the two inch difference from the scope to the rifle barrel, steadied himself on the ping pong table and put a crease right through the other edge of the table. I don't think Dad ever knew how that crease got there.

One day Pen brought home a 45/70 rifle which is an extremely powerful gun. The recoil would bruise your shoulder. He fired that down in the basement when the folks weren't home and it knocked the bullet trap back several feet. He didn't try that again in the house.

Kids were allowed to go hunting when they were fourteen years old. Dad agreed to take Pen hunting on the first day of the season. While Dad was having his regular martini and helping to fix some food he said to Pen "take the gun apart, go up and get the old black powder shells out of my drawer, bring them down and we'll make certain they still fit properly in the gun." One had swollen and got stuck in the barrel. Dad said "now get the ram rod and push the shell out from the other end before you do anything else and don't put the gun back together again". Needless to say, Pen was so excited about going hunting that he forgot.

He was sitting in the dining room, just off the kitchen with the gun across his lap. Just after I walked across in front of him he pulled the trigger and the gun went off with a huge boom. Dad stepped back and said"Jesus Christ the God Dammed kid blew a hole through the wall".

There was about a six inch hole in the dining room wall and a ten inch hole in the living room wall and the whole back of the couch was ripped out and it was pushed about two feet from the wall. One of Pen's friends, Harold Westby, happened by at that time and the scene struck him funny so he broke out laughing. Dad was so angry he picked him up and threw him out the back door. Pen didn't get to go hunting that year.

Chapter VIII

Elementary School Years

I started in the third grade at Willard Elementary School which was within walking distance from home, about a mile. I became fast friends with many boys, red headed Joe Thompson, my favorite, Bill Marx, Jack Rohrbach, Don Fiedler, and many others. School was no problem for me. I always received good report cards with high marks in everything. The school system there was tops in the state. Elementary schools in those days didn't offer lunch rooms. We all walked home during the one hour lunch break and ate at home. If for some reason a mother might be gone for a day one teacher on a rotating basis would allow a few kids to brown bag their lunches to her room. Generally speaking women were not yet a part of the workforce so they were home to provide lunch for the kids.

A neighbor, Herb Nowack who was one year older than me spent a lot of time with me building huts in the woods at the end of the street. In the summer we would daily take our axes and hammers etc. and cut down trees and assemble a log house with bunks at each end. We even had a heater and a little Bunsen burner cook stove. We found plenty of tar paper at construction sites to cover the roof and make it water proof. It would last until some other kids found it and destroyed it. Then we would find another location and build another one.

I became interested in baseball and football so joined little league. I always wanted to be where the action was so I wanted to be a catcher. I felt that the catcher can direct everyone where they should be standing, he tells the pitcher what pitch to throw, he aggravates the batters, and he talks up enthusiasm to the whole team. That was for me. I went to the library and read a book on catching by Yogi Berra which helped me a lot. I became a team leader and did a good job at catching.

In the fall a lot of us liked to play tackle football. We each got helmets and shoulder pads and whatever sweatshirt we could find to put together a rag-tag team. We chose teams each day and played against each other because little league football had not yet been developed. In the sixth grade Joe and I went down to the sporting goods store and talked to "Shorty" who sold the kids sporting goods. We told him we had a football team but no one to play against and asked if he knew of any other elementary schools that were in that situation. He said he would get back to us and he did find several other elementary schools that could put together teams so we started playing at home and away.

One day when Herb and I were about to go into the woods Dad stopped us. Apparently a dead man had been found at the back end of the woods. Later the newspaper said that his stomach had been razor cut crossways, both wrists cut, and his throat cut. The police ruled it a suicide but the paper questioned that a person could lose so much blood so fast and be able to do that much damage to himself. A person who lived on the hill said he heard two cars pull up in the middle of the night and then one left. The ruling of suicide must have saved a lot of investigative hours. It certainly got our attention and made us a little squeamish about going into the woods.

I used to go out with my flashlight at night to catch night crawlers for fishing. Pen and his buddies fished down at Huffman's Pond all of the time and I wanted to get in on the action. When he saw me going down to fish he complained that I wouldn't let the little ones go that I caught etc. etc. I brought home a four pound bass, much larger than any fish he and his friends had ever caught. Pen wasn't home so Dad told me to put it in water in the bath tub. When Pen and his friends came home Dad commented that I had caught a bass. Dad baited them and they grumbled that I should have thrown the little fish back. He said "Paul go get the fish and show it to them". There eyes about popped out of their heads. That week my picture was in the sporting section of the paper with my huge catch.

The war with Korea had broken out and I looked forward to watching our progress on the map on the front page of the newspaper each day. That was the last war where there were realistic measurable front lines.

I also watched the sports page to see where the Yankees were. I was an avid Yankee fan and from 1949 to 1953 they won five straight World Series Championships. The man who owned Glenross ice cream knew what a fan I was and always bet me a quart of ice cream. I won each year and sometimes ate it all by myself while walking home from his store.

In those days there were three New York teams, the Yankees, the Dodgers, and the Giants. Since then the Giants went to San Francisco and the Dodgers to Los Angeles.

Either the Dodgers or the Giants played against the Yankees each of those years and it was called the "Subway Series" reflecting the fact that the only travel the teams had to do between opposing stadiums was by subway.

I had the good fortune to attend one of the World Series games in Yankee stadium with Mom. I saw Mickey Mantle, Gil McDougald, Allie Reynolds, Yogi Berra and Phil Rizzuto play and Casey Stengel manage the game. Hank Bauer hit a home run to win the game for the Yankees.

I went to a lot of Yankee ball games and got to see some of the greatest players ever to play the game. I saw Joe Dimaggio who years later Carolyn and I had dinner with, Fireman Joe Page, Satchel Page, Roy Campanella, Johnnie Mize, Jackie Robinson, Bobby Thompson, Larry Doby and many others. I was very fortunate. The men in the neighborhood called me "Little Yogi"

From my earliest days it was drilled into me that one should always be on time. Grandpa said he once fired a secretary for being late. Mom was adamant that we be on time. And Dad would scold Pen because he was always late. I don't know how many times I heard him tell about the man that ran for the train but got there just as the train left the station. He commented to a person standing there "I guess I didn't run fast enough" To which the man replied "Oh you ran plenty fast, you just didn't start in time". No wonder I am always early wherever I am going.

Like most brothers we were competitive with each other and we had our share of fights which I always lost. I recall one day I got so mad at him I chased him down the street with a baseball bat. He was so embarrassed to be running away from a little guy like me that he finally let me take a swing, stepped back and then decked me. That was the end of that.

Chapter IX

Maine

Starting when I was nine or ten we went to northern Maine on vacation to fish for Smallmouth Bass... It was a 600 mile drive with no air conditioning in the car. The first time we went we took route 9 out of Bangor headed toward Princeton, Maine. Although AAA mapped the trip for us Rt. 9 turned out to be a 100 mile dirt road through the Maine forest. Not believing we could be routed on such a road we plodded along thinking soon it would turn back into a highway. It didn't. The forest became a great adventure for us with an occasional deer along the way. Dad was very uncomfortable because we were running low on gas. At about 50 miles into it we came upon a gas station with a hand crank gas pump. That got us to our destination.

We went to Maine about six years in a row and had wonderful and memorable times which I think are worth relating.

Our destination was Chet's Camp at Grand Lake Stream, Maine. It was hard to find and was well back off the main road on a narrow entrance road to Big Lake. For our first year we were in the cabin on the point which was their most rustic cabin. It was about 300 yards from the other five cabins and the main house where you could eat with advance notice if you chose to do so.

When Chet White, the owner took us down to our cabin he explained that there was an out house but to be careful at night because there were a lot of bears around. He would bring us ice for the ice box on a daily basis and would bring plenty of wood for the wood stove and pot belly heater. He would deliver our boat the next morning because there was to be a storm in the night and he wanted to protect his boat. It turned out the storm was the tail end of a hurricane and we listened to the lake lap along the shore next to the cabin most of the night. We had kerosene lanterns and fortunately, we had brought flashlights.

Heeding the warning about the bears at night we chose to avoid the outhouse and to go in pots rather than to venture out at night. Mom found some pots in the cupboard which she put under the bed for us to pee in during the night. Little did she know the pots had holes in the bottom so there was a mess to clean up in the morning.

Regardless of the rustic inconveniences we had a fantastic time. We fished a lot and caught a ton of bass which Mom cooked on the wood stove for lunch and dinner. Occasionally we would go to the main cabin for dinner. Chet's wife Paula was a great cook. That was a real treat.

I won't bother with year by year accounts of our activities but will simply hit some of the highlights.

Most years the Grandparents Meeker went with us. In the evenings the adults would all play bridge and Pen and I would fish in the dark off the small dock in front of the cabin. It was fun to cast surface lures and listen as the bass slapped at them until they finally found the lure.

The water was very cold as we were way up by the Canadian border. One morning Pen, Dad and I wanted to go fishing early but we had no bait. Dad said let's go out to one of the islands and catch frogs, which was our standard bait, and then we'll fish. This lake was like Golden Pond in the movie with large rocks surrounding the islands. As we approached an island at about six AM with heavy clothes on and shivering in the cold morning air, Dad said "Pen get up in the front and watch for rocks and holler if you see one so I can avoid it". Pen hollered stop but Dad as would be expected ignored him and we ran up on a large submerged boulder.

After unsuccessfully trying to dislodge us with an oar Dad said "Pen, take your pants off and get in the water and push us off". Pen said "I told you to stop, it's your fault, I'm not getting in the water". After a minute Dad said "Paul take your pants off and get us off this rock". Of course I couldn't betray my brother and it was really cold out. I said "I had nothing to do with this; it is between the two of you". After a minute of frustration and awkward silence Dad said ". God Damned kids", took his pants off, got in the water and that was the last we ever heard about it.

One year Pen brought his shotgun and some skeet that we could throw for him. While he was shooting out into the lake area another camper came down to watch him. He happened to be the National Skeet Champion and offered to teach Pen to shoot. Pen became a super star in the sport of skeet shooting to the point where he could break 500 straight with ease and the sport became boring so he quit.

Another year Chet was having trouble with raccoons ravaging the garbage. One night he went out and shot one that weighed nearly 40 pounds. I wanted the tail for my bike so they peeled the skin off and stuffed the tail with salt to dry it out and then tied the end. I kept it for many months but it never did stop stinking.

In the ninth grade some friends and I got into some serious trouble to which Dad had to intervene to keep us from more serious actions against us. The subject was not brought up again until we were in Maine the following summer and he and I were alone fishing about half a mile from shore. Suddenly he said I don't believe you can swim to shore from this far out so perhaps it's time for the two of us to have a little discussion about what happened this spring. It wasn't as bad as it sounds but I clearly learned what he thought and that I had better straighten up. That was Dad's style, he chose the time and place carefully before he let us know who was the boss. I was always an enigma to him because I was very hard headed and not afraid to state my positions. As an example, I remember when I was learning to read there were two words that I just couldn't get right. Dad was testing me with flash cards and I kept making the same mistake. He got so frustrated he said "if you miss that again I'm going to spank you". When the word came up again I refused to speak. He demanded that I answer but I said "I won't, because if I do and I get it wrong you'll spank me. I won't answer". He had to retreat. I eventually did learn to read.

The last time I went to Maine I went without my folks and took my friend Don Fiedler. Of course we couldn't afford a cabin so we took a tent and stopped at Chet's to see where on the lake I might find a place to pitch the tent and to rent a boat. He recommended a place on a sandy beach about six miles away, he rented us a boat, and one of us drove the boat while the other found the place with the car.

We did a good job of pitching the tent and didn't get wet even though it rained hard one night. Chet offered for us to sleep on their porch if it rained but there was no need. We cooked over a campfire, usually fresh fish and fried potatoes. It was great.

Don and I each bought a revolver just because they were available and intriguing. We practiced shooting but we weren't very good and the guns were not the best. Early one morning we had the flaps down on the tent and I awoke to hear someone walking around the tent. I poked Don and we both loaded our guns and laid back to see what was going to happen. We were afraid to open the flap and startle whoever the intruder might be. We both fell back asleep with our guns at the ready and never did find out who was there but we did find foot prints in the sand around the tent. I don't know who was more lucky, us oR the intruder.

We went off one night and tried to meet girls at the Passamaquoddy Indian Reservation but didn't have any luck other than to talk to them and learn too much about the ways of Indians on reservations.

On the way home I decided to cut across Maine, New Hampshire, Vermont, and New York to drive over to Cornell University in Ithaca, New York. I had not been there and wanted to see the campus and to see if I could get an interview. I took them by surprise without an appointment but they eventually worked me in. I don't know what role that played in my later acceptance but hopefully it didn't hurt. I guess it said to them that I was aggressive.

CHAPTER X

Pen

In adulthood, one of Pen's close friends said to me,"When I first met your brother I thought he was the biggest liar that I had ever met. After I got to know him I learned that he can do everything that he says he can and more. He is the most amazing person I have ever met". That in a nutshell was Pen.

Pen's aptitude was in the genius range. Everything that he was interested in came easy to him. Usually once he became highly proficient in something he got bored with it and changed his focus to something else. If it didn't interest him he simply didn't do it.

That was the case with his cello playing. He got bored and stopped playing the cello when he was in his early teens. Schoolwork didn't interest him so it played second fiddle to whatever was his fancy at the time. Usually his grades were in the C to C- range and he quite often went to summer school to get past some failing courses. Somehow he was accepted at N.Y.U. and did graduate with a BA in Business Administration.

Whereas I was very involved in team sports, Pen was only involved in individual sports. He loved to hunt and fish and shoot skeet. With expertise he tied his own flies for fishing. He loaded his own ammunition for shooting. He became a photographer and developed and printed his own pictures. He was good at whatever he wanted to be good at.

I recall that he went into New York City to modeling photo galleries and somehow talked his way into photo shoots of nudes, the pictures of which he would develop in our basement. I watched him do this enough times so that I knew how to do it and when he wasn't home I would find his negatives and print a set of nudes of my own. I hid them under the insulation in the upper attic and they are probably still there, years after all of the models have probably died of old age.

As a teenager, there was a family about two blocks away that was very critical of Pen's character. One fall day when Pen was walking past their house he noticed that the father, who had been burning leaves, had momentarily gone into the house to go to the bathroom, leaving his small son outside. The boy had gotten too close and the fire crawled up his pant leg. Pen immediately tackled the child and patted out the fire with his hands burning himself but saving the child's life. They never bad mouthed him again.

Pen became a motorcycle enthusiast and owned different ones during his teens. He hung around with some other cyclists which raised the eyebrows of our neighbors. They weren't bad guys but they weren't in keeping with the nose in the air standards of some members of the community.

I think Pen's favorite sport was girls. He was very handsome and having a motorcycle was an attraction to the girls. However for most dates he generally borrowed one of the family cars. What a boon to his existence when Dad bought Mom a Nash Ramble convertible, the first car that advertised fully reclining seats. I could see Pen licking his chops. I don't know what Dad was thinking.

Pen never saved money. If he had it, he spent it. When he decided to get engaged, at twenty years old, he borrowed the money for the ring from me. Dad insisted that he pay me interest which he did. And when he got married I gave he and Nancy a television set for a wedding present because I knew he had no money to buy one. Television sets were relatively new and still only black & white.

When Pen went to ask Nancy's father, Art, for permission to marry his daughter he went out for a swim in the ocean with him. Nancy lived in Long Branch, N.J., near the ocean. Both Pen and Art were strong swimmers and swam together often during the courtship. They swam quite far out and Pen said "Art I came this weekend to ask for your permission for me to marry Nancy. If you say yes that will be wonderful, but if you say no I will drowned you". They got married.

Following college Pen went to work for Dad as a salesman in Syracuse, New York. By then Dad was Vice President of Sales for Oneida and his sales manager, Irv Mermelstein had the challenge of supervising Pen. To Pen work was only a necessary pastime until he could get back to whatever interested him at the time. He was a fantastic salesman and no matter what monthly sales budget they gave him he would quickly exceed it and then golf or fish or hunt for the rest of the month.

In his "manufactured off time" he became an excellent golfer playing in the 70s, he learned all of the good fishing holes in Northern New York, he hunted all over the area and kept sufficient game in the freezer for his excellent cook and wife Nancy to provide delicious meals for the entire family.

During my third year at Cornell I lived in a basement apartment with an outside entrance. Cornell was about fifty miles from Syracuse where Pen and Nancy lived. Quite often I would come home from class and find dead rabbits hanging from the water pipes that crisscrossed the ceiling with bloody newspapers spread out underneath to catch the drippings. I never ate one of them but I knew that the black chef at our fraternity loved rabbit meat so I would trade him the rabbits for steaks that he pulled out of the freezer.

At one point Dad and the two other officers of the company, Sam Stein the President and Mal Kimmelman the Vice President of Production, found some way of accumulating a large quantity of cash that could be concealed from the IRS. Dad asked Pen to hold the cash for all three of them in his safe deposit box up in Syracuse for a period of time. When he asked for it back Pen refused to give it to him. Pen reasoned that he took some of the risk so he deserved a cut. At the very least he should have a raise. What a dilemma this was for Dad. He was on the hook for his boss' and his associate's share of the money but his son would not give it back to him. I never knew how it got resolved but Pen did give back the money.

I want to go on record for anyone who happens to read this that I do not condone what Dad and his associates did. Nor do I think Pen was right in his actions. The law is the law and it must be obeyed. Bending the law to the limits of legality to avoid taxation is fine but breaking it is not.

Dad finally talked someone into recruiting Pen away from Oneida because he simply could not control him.

As mentioned above, Pen was an outstanding salesman. He had many jobs in sales with a variety of companies during his career but the same thing happened every time. He would be such a strong salesman that he would be promoted to sales manager and then he would fail and get fired. He simply could not administer or supervise. I would say he was the classic example of the "Peter Principle".

Personality wise Pen was a bold and strongly overbearing individual. Nothing frightened him. He was large, about 250 pounds, and strong as an ox. He always carried a gun and was not afraid to bring it out if someone gave him a hard time. He never shot it at anyone but he certainly got the attention of some men that had some sort of a scrape with him.

He continued to fish and camp all of his life. I recall a picture of him with a bottle of Yukon Jack sitting on a dam in Canada about ten feet from a bear offering a swig from the bottle to the bear. He had a fishing boat that he took out into the turbulent seas of the Atlantic to get bluefish or sharks. He was well known for his skills at fishing and managing a boat in dangerous waters.

Pen could talk your ear off but it was all with affection and probably with a hidden desire for recognition and love.

When he was first married, he and his father-in-law went duck hunting in South Jersey. They stopped for beer and oysters on the half shell in some bar. Both of them caught hepatitis C from the oysters. About thirty years later they both died within months of each other from the continuing affects of the disease. Pen was fifty four, always loved his daughters and would have loved to see all of his grandchildren.

As brothers we fought a lot when we were little, like animals staking out their territory or perhaps competing for the attention of our parents. As teenagers he took me under his wing and taught me a lot, many things I probably shouldn't have been taught at such an early age. We camped and fished and hunted together with his friends, which again was more mature exposure than I should have had. As adults we took somewhat different directions in life but we always wished each other the best. I was appalled by some of the things he said and did but I respected him, admired him for his many talents, and I loved him. He was my brother.

CHAPTER XI

Junior High School
Grades 7 – 9

I'm not sure why I was always motivated to earn money, but I was. It might have been my distaste for asking my father for money or it might have been his distaste for being asked. Either way, I liked to have my own money in my pocket whenever I needed it.

Even in elementary school I looked forward to snow so that I could go door to door and get jobs shoveling driveways and sidewalks. That was hard work. I also started mowing lawns in about the fifth or sixth grade. When I first started mowing lawns we did not have a power mower so it wasn't as easy as it is today. Eventually dad bought a reel type self propelled mower that I could use. What a difference that made.

When a new family moved in I always went to their door, introduced myself, and tried to get them to hire me to do their lawn. One year The Hutchinsons moved in next door and I was hired. Apparently I made a good impression because years later when I needed a job, Mr.

Hutchinson hired me to start as a salesman for Maxwell House Coffee in Sarasota, Florida. It never hurts to leave a good impression.

I took great pride in my work, always crosscutting the lawns and edging and trimming. I quickly built up a client list of about five houses on our street and one or two on nearby streets. Later in high school when I was working a regular job I hired other kids to mow the lawns for me and I took a cut of the fee. I always went around to check on their work when I got home.

I mentioned earlier that our community was very particular about the maintenance of their yards. Having crabgrass was about as big a sin as one could have. There was a house on our street owned by a Mrs. Moynahan, a widow, whose lawn was nearly all crabgrass. It drove the neighbors crazy because they were convinced that the seeds blew into their yards causing them to dig out the crabgrass by hand for many hours each year.

One day Dad came home with an article about a new product developed by O. E. Linck Chemical Company called Di-Met. It was reputed to kill crabgrass without damaging the good grass. I asked him if he could go to the laboratory and see if he could buy me a gallon.

I went to see Mrs. Moynahan and offered to rid her lawn of crabgrass for $100. Dad got the chemical for $16 and I bought a tank sprayer and some string. I lined the lawn with the string so that I would not overlap, sprayed the grass, waited a week for it to die and then raked it out. She ended up with a fine lawn when the good grass thickened and filled in the open areas and I ended up with my pocket full of cash. That was a lot of money in the early 50s.

I also started cutting and selling cordwood with my friend Don Fiedler. I went to the hardware store and bought a two man saw to make the job easier. Chain saws had not yet been invented. That was hard work. I recall after a storm the two of us agreeing to cut up a large tree that had fallen in someone's yard. I guess we got tired and careless and unfortunately I chopped off the tip end of Don's finger. He jumped back without a sound and gradually pulled his glove off until he saw his finger. Then he started howling and jumping around like crazy. I retrieved the tip of his finger, went to the owner of the house and we put it on ice and she took us to the hospital. They didn't sew it back on. That was the end of our wood cutting career.

As I accumulated a little bit of money, Dad got amused and started to bring me financial reports of different companies. I would look them over and he would invest the money for me. I made a little bit of money, nothing great, but it was an introduction for me into the world of business.

Throughout junior high school my friends and I continued to go camping. We usually went to Lake Surprise which was an hour's drive away to the base of a mountain and then a strenuous hike to a lake well hidden at the top of the mountain in New York State. We would often stay for four or five days at a time with our guns and fishing equipment and a knapsack full of Dinty Moors Beef Stew, and Franco American Spaghetti which we heated over an open fire. We swam and bathed in the lake and never saw another person when we were up there. We never caught a fish up there either.

Business ethics in those days were not what they are today. Dad was VP of sales and for many years he had maintained some business relationships by under the table financial incentives. One day the head buyer for his largest account retired and a young man who appeared to have more rigid standards took over. Dad was very afraid he would lose the business because he really was not as competitive as he should have been. For some time he and Mom would entertain this young couple in New York City. One day Dad said to him " You two are so much younger than we are I know that you would have more fun going to the places that are more for your age and we could go to our own style places. I am obligated to entertain you and happy to do so but both of us would have a better time if I just gave you what it would cost for Broadway tickets and dinner a few times a year and let you entertain yourselves. The guy bit.

Dad told that story at dinner one night and said triumphantly "I got him". That entrapment story and statement troubled me so much that in my own mind I said I will never let someone say about me "I got him". I never forgot it and I am certain that it had some influence on me throughout my squeaky clean career. The influence that parents have upon you is not only for what to do but sometimes for what not to do. One has to use his own judgment.

For some reason I was always a champion of the minority or the less advantaged or the weaker person. I didn't like to fight but did so to defend someone who was being picked on or to defend the reputation of a girl etc. One day while hitch-hiking home from school an older boy started picking on my friend that was thumbing with me. I defended Don, whose father had just died, and somehow got into a horrible fist fight. It lasted a long time and I pummeled the kids face and head. Unfortunately he ducked a few times and I hit him in the forehead breaking my hands. The fury of the fight went on until some lady stopped her car and told me to get in. The other kid had his bike there.

When I got home my fists were covered with the kid's blood and twice their normal size. Dad was home recovering from a slipped disc and wasn't amused by the look of my fists. He just said "I thought I taught you to keep your fists tight". Later, against his wishes, Mom took me to the doctor and both fists were almost compounded in two places. I had casts on both hands halfway up my forearm with only my thumb and forefinger showing.

I healed in about three weeks.

I continued to play organized baseball in the Babe Ruth League. Early in the spring when it was still cold I was notified that I would be on Mr. Hetherington's team which was always the team to beat. He called a practice on a rainy cold day and without any warm up had me trying to throw down to second base. I quickly threw my arm out and valiantly struggled to get the ball there but couldn't.

A week or two later, during which I had broken my fists, Mr. Hetherington saw me on a corner down town and stopped to tell me that I had been traded to what would likely be the last place team. I was devastated. This was more than a trade, it was a rude rejection.

We played Mr. H's team three times that season and beat them every time. I knew in the first game that he would try to steal every base he could thinking I had no arm. In the first inning I threw out a runner stealing second with a perfect throw. Then I brushed aside a batter and threw out a runner trying to steal third. Then I blocked the plate and put out a runner coming home holding them to no runs and being responsible for all three outs. That was my proudest moment in sports. Our three victories prevented his team from winning first place. Years later he confided to Dad that the worst coaching decision he had ever made was to trade me.

Chapter XII

High School

High school started with football tryouts. Even though I was skinny I made the team and played center and linebacker. In those days you could play both ways. I played first string on the JV team and played on the varsity team throughout high school. Unfortunately, as much desire as I had, my 150 pounds didn't keep me on the first string for the junior and senior years. Our team went undefeated throughout the three years which was unheard of. Football was hard work, discipline, and true grit. Running mile after mile in the summer, to stay in shape, to late season practices when the ground was frozen and each fall was painful, this was a work of determination, commitment and pride to never say I quit. I'm still glad I did it but I wish I had more time on the field of glory on Saturday afternoons.

I started dating my first real girlfriend in the eighth grade and dated her throughout high school. We were very serious and together all of the time. I took her to Yankee ball games, the New York theatre and dinners, and we went to all of the dances. I even had jewelry specially designed for her. In the summer following high school, while I was away, she found greener pastures. Although it was devastating at the time, my life would have taken a different course had that not happened and I would not have enjoyed the blessed marriage and family that I have today.

Ridgewood High (RHS) was a good sized school, our graduating class being nearly 500 students. College recruiters descended upon RHS because of the high educational standards it had and probably too because of the students coming from well to do families who could pay tuition.

We had lots of dances every year with many of them being formal. I had both summer and winter tuxedos for the dances. We always gave our dates corsages for each dance having them delivered by the florist.

In the tenth grade I went to a large florist that was off the beaten track and made this proposal. "All of the boys buy corsages for their dates for the dances. Most of them walk home through town past your competitor's stores and not past you. Why don't you give me an order pad and a price list and let me take orders during lunch hour and you give me ten percent commission and my corsage for free?" They liked the idea and I kept the job throughout high school. I often sold twenty or thirty orders for a dance.

The florist was named Schweinfurth and they were so impressed by my efforts that they offered me a job after school and full time in the summer which I took except for football season. My work was in the greenhouses in the winter and also in the fields in the summer. This was a good education, adding to the plant knowledge that I had gained from Mom and Grandpa. Sometimes when it came time to rip out a large bed of flowers for a new planting I might gather five or six dozen carnations and drop them off at my girlfriends house.

The legal drinking age in New Jersey was 21 but in nearby New York (about 20 miles) it was only 18. From the time we were 15 we all knew which stores didn't bother about age and when we got driver's licenses at 17 we made regular trips to the bars in New York. The drive-in movie in Spring Valley, New York was a popular place as long as it had the same movie to report on when we got home as the local theaters. We could pick up a six pack and enjoy an evening alone in the car with a good movie. Enough about that.

I developed a whole new set of friends while in high school. I didn't lose my old ones but added new ones. Rich Poggi, an Italian boy whose father had been injured in the war which left them dependent upon his mother's income as a store clerk. Joe, another Italian boy who lived in Fort Lee where all of the mafia bosses lived. Joe's father was clearly big time mafia. Police would stop Joe for speeding and plead with him not to speed admitting that they could not give him a ticket and not wanting to have to tell his father. We hung out at Joe's house often and when we had parties some of his dad's body guards who had been old soft shoe guys would entertain us. Mom and Dad were always unhappy when they knew I had been over there.

Most of Rich's family lived in Englewood in a large apartment building owned by his grandmother. She was from the old country. She had a huge vegetable garden that Rich and I would turn over for her every spring. Lots of Rich's uncles and aunts lived in the same apartment building and they would all get together at the grandmother's apartment every Sunday for dinner. I was always a welcome guest. Sunday dinner went all afternoon. There was always a meat dish and then a pasta dish, and then perhaps a leg of lamb, and on and on. There also was always home made wine that flowed liberally. The conversation and laughter were a joy. What a happy family.

Rich's whole family chipped together to send him to college and he was my roommate freshman year and at other times. He became a successful veterinarian and I still communicate with him today, fifty years later.

When I turned seventeen I bought my own car, a 1952 Ford Custom. I was one of the only kids to have a car but as they say "I earned it". I went everywhere. Gas ranged between twenty and thirty cents per gallon depending on when there were price wars.

I was a very independent child. With my folks not having been to college I didn't seek much advice from them and they did not probe deeply into what I was doing. I probably wouldn't have told them anyway. I applied to Cornell and to Rutgers as a safety valve. Dad had a friend who graduated from Cornell and asked him to write me a letter of recommendation which he did. I was accepted at both colleges and chose the Cornell College of Agriculture. I'm not sure why but that is where I went. Students of agriculture, the same for pre-vet, (Rich Poggi) were required to spend forty work weeks on farm properties for practical experience in the summers. Rich and I went together to Snedekerville, Pennsylvania, a nothing town that is not even on the map, to a dairy farm of about fifty head of Holstein cows. What an education that summer became.

Graduation from RHS was a formal affair. All of the boys wore summer tuxedos and the girls wore full length white formal gowns and each carried a dozen red roses. To a cadence step we descended from the school through the campus to the football field which had been filled with decorative trees, bleachers, large stage etc. We each passed through to receive our diplomas after appropriate speeches. It was a magnificent affair.

CHAPTER XIII

Lessons of Influence

It seems appropriate that I pause for a moment to reflect upon some of the lessons that my exposure to this point had taught me. As one goes through the school system, he or she learns lots of factual, and some not so factual, information that we store in our brains for future recall and use. Of even more importance is the exposure to family and friends and others that leaves indelible memories that formulate the adulthood character that we develop. Those lessons don't stop at high school but go on throughout life. However, the foundation of ones personality and character, I believe, is established by now.

The following are some of the issues that I had strong feelings about when I graduated from high school.

Honesty.

Mom and Grandpa Meeker drilled this into me so much that to this day I have difficulty even sugar coating comments. Throughout my career peers and bosses have commented that they always knew exactly where I stood on issues. I presented facts and issues and I faced facts. Sometimes people didn't like what they heard but they knew what I thought.

Teamwork.

Having played competitive sports throughout my childhood I had grown full appreciation for the concept of working with each other in cooperation for the benefit of the team rather than to benefit the self. Sitting on the bench during Saturday's football games was not the role I wanted to play but I knew that without a strong second string the first team was nothing.

It often occurred to me during my career, that the so called "glass ceiling" that prevented women for reaching the top in the workforce was caused less by prejudice than by the failure of society in those days to have girls play in competitive team sports. They simply did not have that opportunity to learn about teamwork and leadership and therefore were less qualified as they rose toward higher positions in business. What a shame. Fortunately today there are many opportunities for girls to participate in team sports and learn those valuable lessons.

Competitiveness.

Mom and Dad were both very competitive. Dad was outwardly competitive and Mom was quietly competitive. For Dad there was no other choice than to win whether it be games or cards or arm wrestling or business or whatever. I'm not saying he was a bad sport because he was not. He just didn't give up and he rarely lost. Some people have a way of turning defeat into victory and I think that of Dad.

As I look back I would say that my own philosophy that developed in those early days was play hard to win but if you lose do so with dignity.

Work ethic.

From the early days I recall my father coming home after a long day of work, having dinner, rolling up his sleeves and then setting up the card table with a pile of paperwork to go through. He always carried a package of Chesterfields in his shirt pocket and he would light up and go through page after page until after Pen and I went to bed. And I heard the many hardship stories of his youth and early departure from school to work to support the family and I prided in his successes as he was promoted and we moved to better living conditions. As my competitive nature was noted above I think I always subconsciously competed with my father and my brother to achieve greater success. I worked hard and hard work pays off.

Be on time!

With the exception of my brother, who was always running to catch up, the entire family was committed to being on time or early. How rude it was to keep someone else waiting. If someone else could arrive on time he or she should not have to wait for you to show up. As mentioned earlier Grandpa Meeker fired a secretary for being late. Think about a committee or board of ten or twelve people all sitting around waiting for someone to show up. Even if it is only ten minutes, when multiplied by ten people it is more than an hour and a half of man hours wasted. I never forgot their feelings about timeliness and am nearly always early but never late. One might not be openly criticized for being late but I assure you bosses have long memories and don't like to wait.

Integrity.

One grows up with certain beliefs about what is right and what is wrong. Most of this comes from religion whether it is through formal exposure or through the standards learned from religion by our elders. No matter what religion we prefer, they all fall back on well defined right and wrong and are in general agreement. Live by accepted standards of integrity.

Own yourself.

I mentioned earlier the story about Dad at the dinner table saying about the young buyer "I've got him". I think of it to this day. During my career I turned down many opportunities that were very tempting but had I succumbed to temptation I would not be able to sit here with pride and write this document for my children and grandchildren to read. Live your life so that if your children were watching they would be proud of you. Never allow yourself to become so indebted to someone that you would compromise your ethical standards or your judgment.

Chapter XIV

Snedekerville, Pennsylvania, 1958

Rich Poggi and I were not exactly city slickers but we were a far cry from farm boys. Cornell had required forty weeks of farm credits so we accepted an assignment to work at a dairy farm in Snedekerville, Pennsylvania. This farm was really out in the country. There was not even a town. There was a Tasty Freeze out on the highway which the farmer's wife thought was the greatest thing going but that was about it.

The family we lived with was Roland and Mary Osborne and their eight year old son Rollie. We were lodged in the attic which had little ventilation and was hot as Hell. Pay was $75 per month for which we worked about 77 hours per week. Of course board was included but she was one of the worst cooks that I ever ran across. Rich would often eat what I didn't and then when we went out to round up the cows for evening milking he would have to stop by the stream and throw up.

When I left for the farm, My Grandfather Meeker started writing to me. He was a skilled writer and very knowledgeable in many subjects. Over the years I saved fifty nine of his letters which I have catalogued in a notebook for the enjoyment of others. I think parts of the first letter are worth recording here.

Thursday, June 17 1958

"...There are some things about farming not contained in text books which you should know in advance.

Rudyard Kipling's observation that "The female of the species is more deadly than the male" has not been seriously questioned but he was referring to the human species. His rule does not apply to the bovines. A bull is the most treacherous, most powerful, and fastest animal on this continent. Should you have occasion to go into a pasture containing a bull do not go far from a fence that you can vault quickly. Several farmers are gored to death each year by unexpected attacks from bulls.

Another danger is kicking horses. Do not pass behind within reach of a horse that has a tendency to kick. If you are leading a horse by the bridal or halter and walking beside him keep your distance or he may step his whole weight on your foot.

In case you should milk a cow with a tendency to kick keep your left knee in front of and next to her right hind leg. She has to bring the leg forward before releasing the kick. When you have tried to milk a cow, balanced on an old fashioned one legged low milking stool and holding a 12 quart pail between your knees, one of which is guarding against an unexpected kick, and your face is being pounded by the cow's switching tail, you will have less respect for these circus equilibriants. However you will probably not be called upon to milk by hand unless some stripping is necessary after the milking machine and stripping is not a job for an amateur.

There are many tasks on a farm that require brute strength. Do not try to lift or move a heavy object quickly or without getting firmly and comfortably set for the exertion. Make haste slowly. A hernia can easily result from trying to lift from an awkward position or from trying to lift too heavy a weight.

Should you use a sythe it is quite essential that the handles on the sythe be adjusted to your height and swing for good and comfortable work. The farmer can do this for you. It is very tiring to use an ill fitting sythe for any length of time but not so if it fits.

A whiffle tree is not a species related to the whippoorwill.

A stone boat is not for use on the lake.

It's the still pig that get's the swill.

If you watch the rooster crow you will know why he is called a cock. As a kid I used to watch the rooster get cocked for his clarion call and as the first sound came forth I would shy a stick at him just to hear the ignominious wind up of his voice.

I don't suppose any farmer now has a flail. Should you find one let it lie or you will have bumps a phrenologist can't read.

There is a great deal to be learned about the handling of hay or grain with a pitchfork. Modern machinery has made personal skill along this line less important, but it was recognized and appreciated sixty years ago. The man who could unload a load of hay by hand in from six to ten minutes was respected. It meant that every forkful on the load had been as accurately arranged and placed as a brick layer places his bricks.

Well so much for the farming question......"

Grandpa wrote like that often which is probably what caused me to take interest in my own writing skills. Back to the farm.

We worked hard. We milked about thirty five Holsteins many of which had not been cared for properly and required hand stripping which was very tiring. Frequently the cows would get pink eye or mastitis which Rich and I would have to treat. Mastitis was treated by injecting penicillin into the utter. Milk from that cow was required by law to be thrown away for two days after such injections to prevent the antibiotic from reaching people who were subject to allergic reactions. Roland would not hear of it and told us to divide the milk from that cow between lots of milk cans so the dairy that processed the milk would not find it.

Most days we either mowed hay or picked up bails of hay and stacked them in the barn. Once the hay had dried in the field Roland would run the bailer, his wife would drive a tractor towing a hay wagon and Rich and I would take turns with one of us walking and throwing the heavy bails up onto the wagon and the other riding the wagon and stacking the bails. There was an art to the stacking. Bails had to be placed properly so that they would tie in with each other and could be stacked five high and squared. Then we went back to the barn and had to throw it up into the loft and one of us had to stack it up there.

The bailing twine was hard on your fingers. When Rich and I would wake up in the mornings we laughed that our hands were so swollen that our fingers were out straight and we had to push them to get them to work properly.

Sadly I recall one of the dogs having a litter of puppies. Once they were weaned the farmer wanted me to put them in a burlap bag with some rocks and drop them in the stream. I refused so he did it himself. That was a hard reality of farm life for me. Hopefully not all farmers are as cruel

Later in the summer Roland wanted to take his family on a week vacation. That was a real compliment because farmers don't just trust anyone with their livelihood. He left me in charge but with a rotten assignment. For years prior to artificial insemination he had kept a bull in a large room in the bottom of the barn. He had never cleaned it. The manure was about three or four feet high and tightly packed, crusted on top but soaked with stale urine deeper into it. He wanted the room cleaned out by the time he got back.

I worked the inside with a pick axe and pitch fork throwing it out through a window. Rich worked outside throwing it onto a manure spreader (honey bucket as they were called) and then driving each load up into the pastures to spread it around. It was back breaking labor but we got the job done.

I learned a lot about Holstein, Jersey, and Guernsey cows, and the many different forage grasses, and how to run the heavy machinery. I learned a lot that was only good for interest and casual conversation. I learned I didn't want to be a dairy farmer.

In the milk house there was a large cooler filled with water in which we placed the filled milk cans after each milking was done. Every day or two the dairy would come and pick up the full cans and leave us clean empty cans. The water in the cooler was so murky with old milk etc. that one could not see into it. Rich and I used to submerge beer in it so that the farmer couldn't see it. Often after dinner when we finished the night milking we would have a beer.

On the night before we left for home Roland came out to make certain that we had not been careless, knowing that we would not return. We reached down into the cold water and offered him a beer. He took one, drank with us but didn't say anything about it. I could tell he was surprised.

If I learned anything of real value through this experience it was that there are ways to run a business and ways not to. Risking the health of others (the penicillin) for a little profit was stupid and selfish. Farming is not green fields with placid cows chewing their cud; it is dirty, hard, demanding work. About myself, I learned that I can endure the most challenging of work, both mentally and physically and I won't quit.

Chapter XV

Polio

While I was tending the pastures in Snedekerville, apparently my long time girl friend was cultivating greener pastures of her own. The "Dear John" letter came as quite a shock. I could not convince her otherwise and was crushed.

A few days after our return Mom and I went to visit Pen and Nancy who were living about twenty miles away in Elizabeth, New Jersey. Dad was in Minneapolis on business. We all went bowling and had dinner together. I began to feel sick so we went home.

I got progressively worse through the night and during the next day. In those days family doctors came by the house when you were sick. Dr. Keating came three times during the day after only being called once in the morning. About nine o'clock at night I told Mom the pain in my head was too much for me and asked her to call the doctor to see if he could give me a shot to make me sleep. He simply said an ambulance is on the way.

Mom had the neighbor follow us and she piled into the ambulance with me. They by-passed the local hospital and took me to Bergen Pines, a large regional facility. On approach the driver inquired which building and Mom later told me he was really mad because they directed him to building #5, the infectious disease hospital. Apparently Dr. Keating lied and told the ambulance company that I had a ruptured appendix because they were not allowed to transport infectious diseases. Now they had to fumigate the ambulance before it could be used again.

Once in the hospital a lot of medical people came in and the doctor said we are going to do a spinal tap. At that point I didn't care if they killed me because I was in so much pain. He called in eight or ten people who actually laid on me to prevent me from moving while they did the tap. Afterward they gave me a shot to put me out for the night.

When I awoke there was a nurse sitting in my room. She said well you made the front page of the morning paper. She said you are the first polio case in the county this year. Of course by law they could not publish my name because of the hysteria that always surrounded potential exposure to polio cases. I had taken the first Salk vaccine shot but at that time it took three shots over a period of time for immunization.

I asked what happens now? She replied well you just lay still and the next twenty four hours will determine how bad it will get. I had always been an optimist and one of those teenagers who knew they were invincible so it was clear that I was not going to be paralyzed. Clear to me anyway. It scared the crap out of my folks.

I was in the hospital about ten days and I saw a lot of things that I will never forget. The day after I arrived, a man and his young son were admitted to the room across the hall with both being paralyzed from the waste down. I could see the father and tried to talk across the hall to him but he was not interested. One day I could hear him ask the doctor how this was going to affect his married life. After the doctor told him it would have no effect on his sexual activity he was in a better mood and began to communicate. The worries he must have had as a father and bread winner with a paralyzed child, and being paralyzed himself. I often wondered what ever happened to him.

I wheeled myself around in a wheel chair, which the staff required, so I could visit a lot of the other patients. There was a pretty woman there in an iron lung that had been there for twelve years. She got polio when she gave birth to her daughter who now came to visit her. Her hair hung straight down from about four feet high almost to the floor and was brushed every day by the staff or her daughter. She could move nothing and the pulsations of the iron lung worked as a diaphragm breathing for her. There were others, but you get the idea, it was a moment of realization about the down sides of life for the less fortunate.

I got out weighing 128 pounds at my current height of six feet. Dr. Keating tried to talk me out of starting college that year. He said "your brain is swollen, your concentration will be minimal, you will have severe headaches any time you exert yourself and you are likely to have difficulty with your grades. He was a pretty smart guy and was right on all counts. Of course I didn't listen to him. I wanted to keep up with Rich who was to be my roommate.

I guess the only thing I learned from this is that there are always people worse off than you are. It must have been more traumatic than I remember because even to this day I can not talk about it without getting emotional.

Chapter XVI

College

I was ill prepared to enter college in 1958. Recently out of the hospital, under weight and weak, emotionally drained from what I had seen and crushed by the loss of my long time girl friend. I went anyway.

Rich and I were fortunate and had fantastic accommodations which amounted to a suite with two small bedrooms and a large sitting or study room. We made friends quickly and trudged our way up and down the hills of the Cornell campus to our classes. That was very difficult for me. I was given permission to have a car and to park on campus near my classes. When I called home to retrieve my car I learned that it had been sold. Mom and Dad generously gave me Mom's car and she got a new one. This helped a lot.

Cornell was a very liberal institution. They expected you to be an adult and they treated you like one. Beer was sold in the cafeteria line, attendance was not taken in classes, and your hours in the dormitory were not controlled. New found freedom was more than many students could handle. I must admit it gave me some challenges too.

Classes began well as my high school was so advanced that I had already learned much of what the early lessons were about. I was over confident and less attentive than I should have been.

My advisor was all the way at the other end of the campus, more than a mile away and up the hill. Often when I went to see him he would not show up. I struggled. He was leaving on sabbatical and was more interested in where he was going than in giving me advice. When he scheduled my second semester he loaded me down with twenty one credit hours including chemistry and zoology. It was more than I could handle. I did poorly and was suspended for a year.

That summer I took a job at a spring water company as a driver's assistant delivering those large bottles of water for the water coolers. About three weeks into the job I got a hernia that required surgery and laid me up for the summer.

Dad helped me get into Boston University for the fall semester so that I could earn some credits and stay closer to my classmates. B.U. was a good experience, it was not as challenging as Cornell and I got nearly straight A's. Perhaps the suspension got my attention. With my confidence up and my strength growing I asked for early return to Cornell and was accepted back for the spring semester. I did well but was always saddled with the cumulative grade point average of the first year.

I pledged Alpha Tau Omega Fraternity and became one of the leaders holding different officer positions at different times. Fraternity life was an education in itself.

We wore coat and tie to class and for Wednesday and Sunday dinners. We were moral and ethical leaders on campus. We managed a large house that slept about fifty men. Finances, house repairs, handling disputes etc. was good training. We also partied hard as all parties were full open bar and often we hired bands.

Again Rich and I were required to do our farm credits. We lucked out and accepted an assignment on a cattle ranch in Jackson Hole, Wyoming. That was a wonderful experience which I will cover separately.

All continued to go well until the spring of my junior year. The arts college was experimenting with a new grading system wherein they graded only in fives or tens. If you failed a course with a 59% you were given a grade of 40. The college of Agriculture graded on straight percentage average. Unfortunately I failed an optional modern math course that I took in the Arts College. My 58 average was recorded as 40 and my cumulative was so impacted that I was once again dropped.

I went home in shame. At the dinner table one night when Pen and Nancy were over he made some smart remark about my failure which cut so deep that I swore to him at the table that I would exceed him in everything we do in life. It was a very bitter time. My competitive nerve was stimulated, my pride was hurt, and I vowed that by the time I was thirty I would have been back to Cornell and graduated. I'll cover my senior year later.

The most important observation I made from this experience is that you can never fully appreciate the sweetness of success until you have tasted the bitterness of failure.

CHAPTER XVII

Jackson Hole

Before I continue I would like to tell of my experience on the cattle ranch in Jackson Hole, Wyoming which I mentioned in my college chapter.

Rich and I drove in my car across the country to Jackson Hole. Melody Ranch, where we were assigned, sat in what is referred to as the hole and was surrounded by beautiful snow capped mountains. The days were sunny and hot but as soon as the sun went below the mountains the cold from the snow covered tops fell into the hole and one needed a jacket for warmth. Many mornings we shivered in coats until sun up but as soon as you could see the sun you could remove your coat.

We lived in a small bunk house with two other full time ranch hands, one of which left shortly after we arrived. We ate at the foreman's house. His wife was really a good cook and a lot of fun. We worked hard and she provided plenty of good food. At every meal, even breakfast there was always a freshly baked cake for desert.

After lunch there was always a rest period. What a difference from the farm in Pennsylvania.

Rich and I had chores to do each day but if on the weekend we wanted to get away over night someone would step in and handle them. There were two cows to milk by hand and two hogs to slop and that was about it. There were chickens too but the foreman's son was responsible for gathering eggs and feeding them.

Rich and I often went into town after dinner which is famous as a typical wild west town. We went to the Silver Dollar Bar and drank beer, sometimes too much and too late. Bars could not serve after midnight but when last call was made, whatever you ordered was lined up on your table and you could stay until they were gone. We had fun.

Once again my grandfather sent one of his cherished letters. I quote:

"July 30, 1960

Howdy Partner:

Glad to get your letter. You don't mention how you are progressing on the "draw". I assume you are practicing before a full length mirror. Don't overlook the fact that the farther you are from the mirror the better your chance to beat the mirror to the draw. This of course is due to what Einstein labeled "c" in his famous equation. If you find that the mirror is consistently beating you to the draw you better come back east where it is safer.".

"...You mention prairie dogs. One of my earliest faint recollections is of hanging on to my father's legs while he was shooting at passing prairie dogs from the rear platform of a train to, or from California – about 1886-87." Just imagine at that time taking such a trip across the country.

Sometimes when Rich and I were out too late and hung over in the morning, the ranch owner, Paul VonGontard would take us out to his airplane which was parked on one of the pastures to give us oxygen to sober us up. For that we had to pick the rocks off the dirt runway that he had.

I played on a men's fast pitch softball league a couple of nights per week. I would drop Rich at the bar, go play the game, and then meet Rich for beers.

One weekend we begged for time off and drove up to Yellowstone. We slept on the ground or in the car. One morning in Yellowstone I was sleeping in the car with my feet hanging out the window. Rich was sleeping on the ground on the side opposite my feet. He opened his eyes and underneath the car he could see a bear's feet on the other side. There was a bear sniffing at my feet. Fortunately, he didn't find anything that was very appealing. I couldn't blame him.

We enjoyed ourselves at Melody Ranch so much that toward the end I asked the rancher if I could buy one of his pigs and throw a pig roast for the whole ranch. I said if you provide the beer and the wives bring salads etc I'll roast the pig. I had never done this before, nor had I seen it done. I don't know what possessed me but I did it.

I asked a lot of questions and got a lot of advice. I drove up into the mountains where there were a lot of flat rocks and brought back enough to make a bed for the charcoal. I dug a pit in the rancher's yard and lined it with the rocks. I took the seats off the children's swing set and put a pipe as a spit through the chains and moved it over the fire pit.

One of the family members told me to wrap the pig in chicken wire so that as it cooked and got tender the meat would not fall off the bones. I had to tighten the wire every few hours of cooking as the back fat melted and the wire got loose.

Rich and I shot the pig in the head, gutted it, scalded the hair off of it and took it into town to hang in a cooler for a few days. On Saturday we had one heck of a party. It took all day to cook the pig but I had plenty of help turning the spit. We played bareback broom stick polo and a variety of other sporting contests and I dare you types of things as the beer was consumed.

During the summer we spent most of our days using heavy equipment to mow or stack hay out in the fields. We built huge hay storage areas with surrounding walls to prevent the elk from eating the hay.

The cattle were grazing in the high country during the summer so we didn't run across them. On one cattle drive the rancher's horse got gored by a bull right in the shoulder. It left a gaping hole about six inches deep in his muscle. The horse didn't even fall or throw the rancher. Rich and I got the job of tending to the wound. We had to take a cup of iodine and a paint brush and paint the inside of the hole each day to prevent infection. The horse's skin would quiver each time and he would look at us with wide eyes but he never moved away or gave us a problem. That was a great animal.

At the end of August we left with some of the fondest memories of our lives. We recognized the difference in the quality of leadership between the farm and the ranch. Life and work are what you make of them, not what they make of you.

Chapter XVIII

Lost

Ashamed of having been dropped out of college I didn't know what to do. I needed to get my act together, to find some direction. I sought jobs at many places, some businesses saying I was over qualified, and others saying I needed a degree. I took a temporary position in a garden shop just to put a few dollars in my pocket.

Our neighbor, Mr. Hutchinson, whose door I had knocked on long ago and whose lawn I had mowed for years learned of my plight. He called me and said"if you get your military obligation done I'll hire you as a salesman for Maxwell House Coffee when you get out". How great it is that if you do a good job people remember it and the benefits often exceed the pay that you earned at the time. The seeds of reputation that one plants throughout his life can grow to weeds or, as in this case, to beautiful flowers. It just depends upon the quality of seed that you plant.

I opted for the National Guard because you could serve six months of active duty and then five and a half years of reserve duty. This would allow me to get started on my career quickly. Dad pulled a few strings and I was accepted into the New York National Guard in the Bronx. I now had direction and focus.

CHAPTER XIX

Active Duty

I was quickly sent to Fort Dix in New Jersey for basic training. I found it interesting that at the reception center we had lots of recruits, all having no idea of what to expect. There were lots of college graduates and lots of typical New York City wise guys with the DA haircuts and talking smart and tough. They all hung together the first day and were somewhat intimidating to everyone. On the second day we all had our heads shaved and the bravado of those guys was gone. It is strange what appearance and predetermined images can do to ones mind.

Basic training was strenuous but I enjoyed it. After the fourth week some of us were granted a weekend pass. Before I returned I asked Dad for one of his stashed bottles of scotch and took it back with me. One evening we were told there would be an inspection the following morning. I went into the drill sergeant's room and told him about the hidden bottle. He said go get it and I thought this was really going to be trouble. When I came back he had two glasses and some ice and we drank together. He asked if I could bring back a bottle each time I got leave and of course I could. I got leave every weekend for the rest of basic training.

Aptitude tests help determine what specialty you will have in the service. My math scores were high so I was sent to Fort Sill, Oklahoma for advanced training to become a survey computer for forward observation. This involved locating the enemy targets, calculating the coordinates, and radioing back to fire directional control so they could determine the aiming angles and the appropriate powder charge to use. They would then fire a shell and after the impact I would direct them to fire to the right or left and short or long until they zeroed in and blew up the target. This was fun in practice but very risky in reality

I found army life to be interesting. I enjoyed my time on active duty. I liked the discipline, the organization, the teamwork and the recognition for achievement.

The night before my release from active duty President Kennedy announced the Cuban Blockade. I thought they would not release us because we were so close to war with Russia. All night long the trucks and cannons and heavy equipment rumbled past our barracks until the next morning when we went out and found the fort vacant except for a few people.

We were loaded into trucks and taken into the hills well away from the fort and ordered to dig fox holes for the remaining cadre to use if necessary. When we finished they drove us back and released us.

At the same time Viet Nam was beginning to heat up. How fortunate I was to be able to avoid that war where so many American Soldiers lost their lives.

CHAPTER XX

Maxwell House and Marriage 1962 - 1968

I was home in October and left quickly for my sales representative position with Maxwell House. How lucky can a guy get? I was to live in Sarasota, Florida and work from Bradenton down to Naples and east to Okeechobee.

I arrived in Tampa and was met by Griff Brandon the sales supervisor to whom I would report to and who would train me. We stayed the first week in a fine hotel in Tampa while I was taught the paper work and fundamentals of selling coffee. Griff was originally from Alabama and still was plagued by stupid prejudice. As this was still the heart of the Cuban Missile crisis the Army had housed troops all over Florida. They had in fact taken several of the top floors of the hotel in which we stayed.

One day we were going up the elevator and a black officer stepped onto the elevator. When we got off Griff was livid. He said "they let niggers stay here so I will never stay here again". We moved out. I couldn't believe what I had heard. Here was a military officer defending our nation and Griff because of color could not accept him as an equal.

Griff stayed with me for about three weeks calling on stores and introducing me to wholesale accounts. He was an extremely detailed and organized person. All paper work had to be perfectly done and organized in certain ways. My expense report had to have the receipts attached starting at the back with the largest and working forward to the smallest so that he could thumb through them easily. Every Friday night I was to prepare a summary of all of the calls I had made that week with the results and future objectives for each account. Also I had to enclose my expense report, a schedule by day of which store I would see and what my objective for each store would be for the coming week, and where I would be staying each night. All of this had to be sent overnight delivery so that he had it Saturday morning by 10:00 AM. He was equally as demanding as the army.

I rented a small apartment on the water on Golden Gate Point in Sarasota with a bedroom and a fairly large all purpose room including the kitchen. I registered my transfer at the National Guard Armory and got myself organized.

The sales representative job is also known as missionary sales. It involved keeping our company's name in front of the store manager and trying to convince him to do certain things that might enhance our sales. The name of the game was to get as much space as you could on the shelf, make sure your product was in the best location on the shelf in the coffee department, get special end cap displays, and put up posters and other advertising materials in the store to promote the sale of our products. Maxwell Houses was both instant and regular coffees in a variety of sizes, Sanka coffees and Yuban coffees.

I started at $5600 per year and a company car. Unfortunately at that time air conditioned cars had not been introduced. You can imagine making calls at stores in the heat of Florida, and getting in and out of the locked car, how one looked late in the day. We referred to it as a 2/60 air conditioner which meant two windows down and sixty miles per hour.

The most interesting thing to me was learning the science of supermarket retailing. It had never occurred to me why different products or departments were placed in different locations within the store. The whole objective was to control the flow of traffic through the store, to expose the customer to all of the products and to force the customer past high margin impulse merchandise, thereby increasing sales and profits. The bag of tricks that retailers use is endless.

I had about one hundred stores to call on each month. The rule of thumb was that if you are more than thirty miles from home when you finish the day, stay in a motel. The interstate highway system had not yet reached southwest Florida. That meant all meals were expensed which was great for my budget. The stores were broken up into weekly, every other week and monthly frequencies based upon their perceived potential for sales of our products.

My National Guard acquaintances became very important to me. I became good friends with about five men who had been brought up in Sarasota, knew everybody, and still lived at home. What a perfect match. I had an apartment on the water that was perfect for parties and they knew all of the girls in town and had no place to party. When I left town on Monday morning I knew that when I came back on Friday I would have a date. On Saturdays and Sundays we played beach volleyball at Lido Beach. This was the good life.

Late on Saturday nights I had a habit of stopping at a diner on St. Armand's Key for breakfast. Nearly every Saturday night I would run into a fellow there that was a bank teller. Little did I know that he was also a Baptist Minister. It turned out that he was often using our discussions as fodder for his next morning's sermons.

During Christmas week he invited me to his house for dinner because his wife's cousin Carolyn was coming to visit from High Point, North Carolina. Carolyn was a couple of years older than me, a widow, and the mother of a three year old girl, Debbie. Dinner was on a Wednesday evening after which they got ready to go out. I asked "where is everybody going"? Carolyn said "to church". I said "it's Wednesday"? She replied "yes, they have Wednesday night prayer meeting". I said "why are they going"? To which she replied "he's the minister". My mind raced through many of our Saturday night discussions.

Some months later after one of our Saturday night discussions I decided to attend his church to see what he was like as a preacher. He started his sermon looking at me and strongly saying "I MET A SINNER LAST

NIGHT...." There were no more Saturday night discussions.

I found Carolyn to be very attractive with a wonderful southern accent. She was mature, unlike the many other girls I was dating, she was a school teacher, and she had a calm or recessive personality which seemed to counterbalance my wilder side. She was a good influence on me.

She returned to North Carolina and I visited her at least once in the spring and was able to convince her that she would be better off moving to Florida and escaping the close oversight of her family. Her family was wonderful but they were overly protective of this recent widow and excessively attentive and generous to her daughter, Debbie. The result was a very spoiled child, not her fault, just a result of circumstances.

We dated over the summer during which I was asked to move to St. Petersburg to take on larger account responsibilities. It took some negotiating but I was able to break my Sarasota lease after mentioning that if I could not be released from the lease I would make extra keys and allow my friends to use it for parties etc.

Carolyn got a teaching job in St. Petersburg. We were convinced that our future was to be together and quickly got engaged and scheduled a wedding for August 30. I was always a decisive guy. She took a little convincing. I rented a nice house on St. Petersburg Beach for $75 per month with the provision that I would mow the lawn and take care of it. It was great.

Our engagement caused uneasy rumblings from both of our families. One could almost hear the tom toms beating as the war counsels met to discuss the impropriety of our quick decisions and what they were going to do about it.

Her family was not at all comfortable that she was going to marry a Yankee. They did not share my New York style sense of humor, nor did they find my enjoyment of a cocktail or beer to be acceptable. Surely she could do better.

My folks were no different. How could their son marry an older woman with a child? It must be another one of those loose southern girls. What kind of trouble has Paul gotten himself into now? Prejudice and blind impressions are without warrant and valueless. They simply amount to blind fear of the unknown.

In the midst of the storm arrived another wise letter from Grandpa Meeker. "Dear Paul, They say you are about to embark on the sea of matrimony and I wish you a calm and happy voyage. I think it is an advantage to have a mate who has already learned where some of the rocks and shoals are."

We married August 30, 1963 with long time friend Rich Poggi as my best man and Carolyn's cousin Betsy Swafford, the minister's wife, as matron of honor. No, we did not use the bank teller, Baptist Minister for the service. It was a small wedding with both of our families there as well as some local friends. We spent a long Labor Day weekend honeymoon in Naples Florida at the Naples Golf and Beach Club. We are still married today after forty six years and as strong or more strongly committed than ever.

I wanted to be certain that we were a long term family and therefore immediately adopted Debbie in hopes that she would always feel as an equal member of the family once we had additional children.

I was about as poorly prepared for fatherhood as anyone could ever be. I had never been around small children and in particular, a girl. I was on a high speed train for my career and the enjoyment of my marriage. I had little to no patience for a child who had been so spoiled and who resisted taking any direction from me. To make matters worse, Carolyn had allowed Debbie to sleep with her when there were just the two of them. Upon marriage Debbie could not accept being kicked out of our bedroom and I would have it no other way.

Suffice it to say that we had a rough time for many years. I recall saying to a colleague of mine that my handling of this situation was the greatest failure of my life. Somehow she grew up and has two fine grown up children of her own today and is doing well herself.

Upon marriage our landlord at the beach notified us to get out. No children were allowed. We moved into St. Petersburg proper and rented a home with a pool. We had to be very careful to see that the gate to the pool was always closed.

Within a year I was asked to move across the bay to Tampa so that I could take over a very large key account. On the first day that I walked into the buyer's office I introduced myself and said undoubtedly you have some issues that my predecessor did not finish so why don't you tell me all of the issues and then I will excuse myself, get on the phone and come back when I have all of the answers. She was surprised and grateful. I solved her problems and we got along well as did my sales budget for the rest of my stay in Tampa.

We bought our first house in Tampa. It was in northwest Tampa and we paid $16,500 for it. Under an FHA mortgage we put nothing down and had monthly payments of $106. Most of our neighbors were military families with the men stationed at McGill Air force Base. Viet Nam was still hot and they seemed to be taking turns being deployed. Fortunately none of them were lost while we were there.

With a baby on the way I went out and bought a puppy for Debbie much to the dismay of Carolyn. I thought this would help the relationship and perhaps it did. Karen arrived April 12, 1965.

All went well with our life in Tampa and about a year later I was promoted to account manager and sales supervisor in Jacksonville, Florida. In that capacity I would have the responsibility for Food Fair Stores, Colonial Stores, and two sales representatives, one in Tallahassee and the other in Savannah, Georgia

During my first week, my predecessor, Rudy Ogburn was showing me the ropes while we attended an out of town store opening for Food Fair. Their key executives were there and Rudy ended up buying their dinner and finding women for them. The next day I returned to Jacksonville to meet with Roy Shiflett, my new boss. I said Roy; this is what took place last night. It is okay with me that those things happen but I will not be anyone's pimp. If that is what is expected of me then I will get back on the plane to Tampa with no complaints and you can find someone else for the job. If you are willing for me to handle the job as I wish, then I will do the best I can for you. He said you run the job as you see fit and I did. I made my budgets, developed two sales representatives to be successful and was considered successful myself.

Roy was a little guy who always carried a very large briefcase. We used to joke that he only carried that big briefcase so that he could reach the urinals in the airports. He and I became close in a boss/subordinate way. He gave me good sales training and taught me a lot.

My former boss Griff was a severe alcoholic. One day while in the Jacksonville office Roy received a call that Griff had been killed in an automobile accident in Virginia. He apparently had left early on vacation with his wife and he was driving the company car without approval. She was unhurt. Roy immediately went into his office with Vernicia, his secretary, closed the door, and dictated a predated letter to Griff approving his request to start early on his vacation and to take the company car. This thoughtful gesture protected the insurance rights and the welfare of Griff's widow.

When Roy visited Griff's wife she showed him a name and telephone number of a woman she had found in Griff's wallet. She had quickly concluded that he had a mistress out of town. Roy smartly looked at it and said "oh yes, we had a complaint from someone who found some foreign object in her coffee and I asked Griff to follow up. I guess he didn't get to it yet, let me have the paper and I'll take care of it." That quick thinking preserved the loving memories she had for her husband.

As important as honesty is, sometimes one must be creative if it is for the good of the people involved and not detrimental to others.

Our youngest daughter Laurie arrived January 10, 1967 at the Jacksonville hospital. She had a heart problem, what they called a "blue baby", which worried the heck out of us. Carolyn was still in the hospital after delivery and quite distraught. Uncharacteristic of me, I called our minister and asked him to go see her and to get her thinking in the right direction. He did so and Carolyn's attitude improved immediately and luckily Laurie's condition cured itself too.

In the early fall of that year I was promoted again to staff assistant to the Regional manager for the west coast of the United States. This involved relocation to the White Plains, New York area. We sold our house in Jacksonville for about $30,000. Thinking I could splurge and spend up to $35,000 I called a realtor in Connecticut and asked him to find me something in that price range. His stunning reply was "try another state".

We bought a nice house in Ramsey, New Jersey, about ten miles from my folk's home. Housing was so scarce at the time that we had to wait in line to see houses. Often while waiting in line a realtor would come out and say sorry, the house is sold. My company car had been sacrificed in the move and we could not afford another car so Carolyn was essentially imprisoned at home during the week when I was working.

My New York assignment was to be only for one year after which I would again be transferred back out to a location anywhere in the states to await some other growth opportunity. I didn't like that idea and could see myself being at the whim of some new supervisor and possibly being stuck in some God forsaken location with little escape opportunity if I wanted to leave the company. On top of that, my personal commitment to return to Cornell and get my degree before I reached thirty was still on my mind. I applied to Cornell and was accepted.

On a Saturday morning I visited Dad and standing in the yard told him I was going to return to Cornell. His first concern was how I was going to pay for it. I assured him that I would find a way and that he would not have to contribute. His second concern was that I was nuts. He reasoned that I had been promoted repeatedly, was making a good living, had a family obligation, etc. With Carolyn's support I had made up my mind and we were going.

I was granted a leave of absence from Maxwell House which did not provide compensation but did cover medical benefits. We rented the Ramsey house, put most of the furniture in storage, packed a trailer and headed for Ithaca where we had rented an apartment in a student housing area.

This became one of the most important decisions of my life. Sometimes one must leave security and venture into the unknown if they are going to catapult themselves into loftier exploits.

Chapter XXI

My Senior Year

Failure was not an option! Staying longer than one year was beyond our financial capability. This was do or die.

I was assigned a new advisor, Dr.Wendall Earle. Without question, Wendall made a difference in my life. He was not only my advisor, in a way, he was my mentor. I am eternally grateful for his guidance.

We moved into a student housing complex in which we had been told there were not going to be many females as residents. When I came back from registration the first morning, Carolyn said "There are lots of girls living here, I saw them coming out of different apartments and going down the front steps. She was so naïve. I tried to tell her that those were probably temporary visitors and she recoiled in doubt.

There were some other couples living near us, in many cases the husband was an instructor. Eventually Carolyn got to know some of them. She even earned a few dollars taking care of one of their daughters while her parents worked.

In my class, and assigned to my advisor, Wendall Earle, there were about twenty or more students my age. Wendall supervised a professional fraternity to which we were all invited to join. I did and was immediately elected President.

I also went down to ATO where I was still a member. I announced that Carolyn and I were there for a year; that we could not pay dues, but as married adults we met the schools requirements to be chaperones for their overnight weekends and we would be happy to do so. What a deal for them! And what a deal for us. Great parties! They were very appreciative of our availability. Hopefully our blind eyes did not result in any long term ramifications.

I took several classes from Wendall. The most important was a case study course in which we were to read involved business cases, determine the key problem and the sub-problems, develop potential solutions, and recommend the right solution. Each week we had to write a ten page paper with all of that information solving one case study. I got straight A's in that course as well as most other courses. I had matured, was attentive and determined to graduate. Our financial life as well as my personal pride depended on it.

Wendall invited guest speakers from industry each Friday and we, the fraternity members, were invited to go to lunch with the speaker. I always went and was seated next to Wendall and the speaker. It was great exposure. Often the speaker would inquire as to why I was still in college at an older age. Wendall would just wink and say that I was a very slow learner.

Carolyn and I had no money. We had divided all of what we had by ten months plus the minimal amount for rent we received for our house after the mortgage was paid, and we assumed that when I graduated we would be broke but I would be working for a living again. The pressure was on.

One of the smartest things we did was to take a chest freezer with us that we had bought in Tampa. We shopped every ad and never bought anything that was not on sale. We ate turkey wings, used powdered milk which we mixed half and half with regular milk for the children; we bought every cheap food that we could find. We were dirt poor but life was good.

We enjoyed a good social life because all of my fellow students, many of whom were also married, were just as poor as we were.

My first semester was exceptional, dean's list and straight A's. As I registered for the second semester Wendall suggested that I take an additional class. I told him that I had a job as a motel clerk and could not afford the time. He was surprised that I was financially struggling because he thought I was being supported by Maxwell House. I explained that I was on my own.

The next day he called me in to tell me he had a scholarship for me from The Jewel Companies in Chicago. He said there are no obligations but he would appreciate it if I would interview them when the time came for on campus recruiting. He also said, "Before you talk to them come see me for advice".

This was the year of the great standoff at Willard Straight Hall when the "Blacks" took over the student union building and held it for many days. The campus was an armed camp. Even the puny motel in which I worked was loaded with big name news anchors.

I always had sympathy for the plight of the blacks but this was beyond reason. The destruction of valuable art works and the crude defacing of the building with human feces on the walls and furniture and art work was enough to turn anyone against their cause. Fortunately it ended without bloodshed but I don't know what if anything was ever achieved.

I signed up for interviews with lots of companies that spring. I knew I had a safe landing spot with Maxwell House if necessary so I was a bit cocky.

I prepared a chart across the top of which I had key criteria to be considered. Down the side were the names of the companies I wished to interview. After each interview I filled in the blanks with numerical ratings and totaled my rankings to put some order into my decision making process.

Prior to the Jewel interview Wendall told me that Jewel would hire hundreds of students this year but they have two or three special positions called corporate trainees. He said if they do not offer you one of these don't go with Jewel. He explained that to qualify for one of these positions Jewel required an MBA at the top of your class from one of ten key colleges in the country. He said I realize that you don't have those credentials but I think your work experience as well as your record this year should offset those requirements.

The interview seemed to go well with one corporate representative remaining silent and one doing the interview. At the end they invited me to join them for dinner along with several other students. The silent one was at the other end of the table preventing me from talking to him. As far as I was concerned he was a trainee. He wasn't. While waiting for the parking attendant to bring my car the silent one walked over and said "I'm sorry I did not get to sit near you tonight as I wanted to ask you some questions. I think you are a good candidate but I just don't know if you have the moxey for this high a position". His comment struck me wrong and I quickly responded "I'm here on my own money with a wife, three kids and a dog and if you can't see that I have the moxey perhaps I am interviewing the wrong company." He immediately backed off and asked me not to be offended. I got the job at $15,000 per year starting pay. That was a lot for a BA in those days.

With Jewell and Maxwell house in my pocket I interviewed Carnation Milk. I passed the first interview and was invited to go to New York City for the final interviews at the Waldorf Astoria. This was big time for me and a free weekend. I passed that round of interviews too and when asked what I was looking for in the way of compensation I said $20,000. The man was astonished. He said "how can you justify that when everyone else is looking for $8 - 10 K. I explained my chart and said I already have these offers and they rank higher than you in location and opportunity. If you want me, that is what it will cost". He was incredulous but said I'll try but I don't think this can be sold to corporate. It couldn't. He wished me well and that was a laugh for me. When you have a good fall back position that is secure you can be bold and go for broke.

Speaking of broke, we were flat broke as I approached graduation. Our car broke down and we couldn't afford to fix it. Our only solution was to turn it in for a new car and set the first payment for the month after graduation when I would again be earning money. We bought a Chevy station wagon, our first new car other than the company cars I had in Florida.

Mom, Dad and Grandpa came to graduation. I knew that Dad now would come forth with a good sized check to offset my tuition and help us since we were desperate. When I opened my graduation gift it was a sport coat. I was grateful, glanced at Carolyn and took a deep breath. Carolyn and I have laughed often about this as we were so poor and needed help so badly. I was too proud to ask for help.

This had been and still is one of the best years of our marriage. Struggling to survive with all of the chips on the table can destroy or bring people closer together. In this case it was a binding experience that will always be among our fondest memories.

We headed for Chicago having sold our house in Ramsey, which put a few dollars in our pocket. I had to negotiate with Jewell to get them to pay for our relocation which I could not afford.

My father gave me some good advice at the time. He said the company is not interested in worrying about your housing situation. Make a decision quickly and focus your efforts totally on your work. If you pay a little too much for a house, in a year or two, inflation will have brought you back on track. On a rainy Saturday

I walked through the door to a realtor's office where a half dozen agents were sitting at their desks. I said in a loud voice "Who wants to sell a house this afternoon"? The first hand went up and I described what we wanted and could afford and asked where should my wife and I go to lunch? I'll be back in one hour so be prepared. We bought a house that afternoon.

CHAPTER XXII

Jewel Companies

In 1969 Jewel was the ideal company. It was a conglomeration of about twelve different operating companies functioning independently of each other and competing with each other for corporate allocations of growth capital. Jewel food stores in the Chicago area owned more than thirty percent of the market. Star Markets were strong in New England, Buttrey Food Stores were strong in the Northwest, Eisner in Indiana, Osco Drug Stores throughout the country, Turn*Style Discount Stores in Chicago and Boston, Brigham's Ice Cream Shops in Boston, White Hen Pantry Convenience s Stores in Chicago and several other companies.

Frank Lunding a former chairman had defined Jewel as "Merchants of Empathy" characterizing his view of the way employees and customers should share in the success of a business, not only financially but also in satisfaction, development, security and pride. He structured the organization chart upside down with the front line employees and customers at the top and the chairman at the bottom. He taught a first assistant philosophy wherein your direct reporting relationship was not to be considered your boss but your first assistant and the person to whom you could go to with any problems.

Philosophically management believed that jobs should be developed to fit the skills of the employee rather than employees molded to fit the needs of the job. This encouraged creativity and aggressiveness to grow.

Don Perkins was president of the corporation at the time. He was an affable, brilliant man. He was a Harvard MBA, he was young, and he was down to earth friendly, never taking himself too seriously. He believed in the cutting edge leadership philosophies of the corporation.

The Corporate Trainee Program was one of exposure, evaluation, and mentorship. Candidates were sought from Harvard, Brown, Yale, Cornell, Columbia, Stanford, University of Pennsylvania, Northwestern, and the University of Chicago. Usually one or two candidates with outstanding credentials were selected each year.

New trainees spent a lengthy period of time gaining exposure in basically all positions within one of the companies over a ten week period and then would start with another company for similar exposure. One might pass through six or eight companies before being asked to begin a formal career path in one operating company or another. When it was time to select a company the candidate was asked to express his preferences and then the Presidents of each operating company to which he had been exposed would meet with the Chairman and lay out a proposed career path for the individual. Essentially the Presidents were bidding for the candidate by presenting rapid track growth to maximize the use of the candidate's talents. The bidding of the Presidents was matched with the preferences of the candidate and the Chairman decided the outcome.

Throughout the exposure period and continuing well into one's career there was a sponsor or mentor who guided the trainee, counseled him, and basically helped to keep him out of trouble and progressing as rapidly a possible. This was an up or out program. They paid a premium to get you and they expected a return on their investment. If for some reason you did not fit, you were quickly exited from the company.

MY OWN EXPOSURE EXPERIENCE

Bill Lewis, the President of Turn*Style was my sponsor or my mentor. Bill was only thirty seven at the time, eight years my senior. He was an Iowa farm boy who had gone to work for Osco Drug right out of high school. He was a hard worker and very bright. In many ways he educated himself as he was a quick study in everything.

Bill was a born leader. He believed that one should work hard but should play equally hard. He was never afraid to get his hands dirty and worked with the lowest clerk even though he himself was president of the company. I recall during a Christmas season he and his family were shopping at our Glendale Heights Turn*Style store one evening. Bill noticed that the housewares section was seriously out of merchandise on the sales floor. Upon inquiry he learned that some people had called in sick. He said to the clerk "if I stay to help can you take me home after work?" Of course the answer was yes and Bill took his coat off, sent his family home and worked until nearly two in the morning getting the department back in shape. That is the kind of leadership example that he set.

Bill loved to play golf and was a member of Medinah Country Club, one of the finest clubs in Illinois if not the nation. Inviting employees to play golf with him at Medinah was his way of motivating, evaluating, and counseling people. The way in which a person plays golf tells a lot about his character.

I started my training in June of 1969 in the Jewel Food Stores. On the first weekend Bill called me at the store in which I was working and said what are you working on? I said I am trimming lettuce and cutting watermelons why. He said I'd like to have a counseling session with you at Medinah tomorrow morning if you can be there. He said he would get me excused from the store.

This was my first round at Medinah. I knew how famous it was so I was thrilled to be there and a little anxious as to why I might need counseling already. Apparently he just wanted to give me a break and see how I liked what I was doing.

We teed off with two of his friends with a reasonable wager. It might have been reasonable but it was certainly more than I could afford. I thought to myself that I had never played for that much money before but if Bill was paying for the golf I had to go along with the bet even if I could not afford it. I thought about Lee Trevino's statement that pressure is a $10 Nassau with $5 in your pocket.

I played one of the best games I had ever played. I recall playing the twelfth hole and hitting my tee shot into the rough, dubbing my next shot, chipping out to the fairway and hearing Bill say to his partner, I knew he was not this good, he's falling apart now. Luckily, from about 150 yards out I put the next shot into the cup. I casually said would you mind picking my ball up on your way past. I'll meet you on the next tee. I had read Bill correctly; he liked cockiness in competitive sports. We had a good laugh.

My training took me through Jewel Food Stores, Turn*Style Discount Stores, Country Osco Drug, City Osco Drug (two different operating companies) and White Hen Pantry Convenience Stores. I enjoyed the exposure but was anxious to get into the main stream and to become a productive contributor to the organization.

Bill, nor any of the other Presidents, was not allowed to try to influence me about which operating company I would select to start my career. He called me one day when I was working for Osco and asked me to go to Boston with him so that I could witness the grand opening of one of the Turn*Style Stores. He had two first class tickets which was not normal but I didn't know any better. As we sipped on martinis or "large see throughs" as Bill called them, we mused over paper work.

Bill appeared to be doodling on the cocktail napkin. He casually commented "I have a real problem. This is my organization chart today and this is what I envision it to be in two or three years. My problem is that I don't have enough talent in the staff to fill these vice presidential positions. A bright young guy today could be a vice president in a few years making $35,000 a year." He knew that the chart on that napkin was burned into my memory and that when it came time for me to select a company to work for, Turn*Style would be it. Bill saved that napkin and in three years when I achieved the title and income he showed me the napkin to say that he had lived up to his word.

Bill was not the only one to bend the rules. The president of Osco Drug had Carolyn and me over to his home for dinner one night along with his key officers. They got me cornered in the kitchen and tried the lead pipe treatment to get me to select Osco. I chose Turn*Style.

TURN*STYLE

I started as some sort of department supervisor traveling to all of the stores. Within a month or two I became the buyer of giftware. Added to my responsibilities in the first month was a single gas station in the parking lot of our Turn*Style store in Moline, Illinois. I was to study the gas station business and see how we could use it to build the discount store business and add more stations as soon as possible.

Also added in the third month was an assignment to learn about the retail liquor business, to design, build and open a liquor store, adjacent to the Turn*Style in Moline.

After roughly six months Bill called me into his office and promoted me to General Manager of housewares, giftware, automotive, and appliances. In this position I would cover those categories for the entire chain in New England as well as the Midwest. I protested that there were many people who had been there for years and were more knowledgeable than me. Bill said don't worry about it, I didn't hire you for this job and you won't be in it long.

Being a corporate trainee had its advantages but it also had its disadvantages. Other employees at all levels were jealous of the special favors and treatment that I received. Even vice presidents needlessly viewed me as a threat to their long term ambitions. In some cases roadblocks were put in my way to slow down my progress.

GAS STATIONS

What a crazy business the gas station business was. We had two products, regular and premium. Gasoline sold for 33 and 35 cents per gallon with a gross profit of about a dime per gallon. Since all stations had the same price, volume was dependent on traffic patterns. This was not like other retail businesses wherein one could run an ad with a temporary discount and build traffic. Or was it?

I decided to try some tests. Perhaps I could run an ad offering two gallons of free gas with a $10 purchase from the discount store. I reasoned that if I could get the people to stop for the two gallons they would automatically fill up. Not true, most of them just took the two gallons and were embarrassed when we insisted on washing their windows too.

A gentleman, I use the term loosely, asked to meet with me. He explained that he was the manager of the Quad cities Petroleum Dealers Association. Apparently each gas station was to pay him $100 per year for which he would insure that everyone stayed in line with their pricing. I said there was no way that I could expose our corporation by participating in a program like that. He advised me that I should not screw around with the prices or the other stations would undercut me in a price war. I told him I could give the gas away with corresponding sales from the discount store so don't try to control me.

I ran a few quarter page ads sometimes offering one day sales of fifteen or twenty cents per gallon. Traffic was in line at our station all the way around the back of our store. For competing stations that met the price, their traffic backup went out into the streets and the police stopped them because they were blocking traffic. I'm sure they were frustrated and furious. They paid for price protection and their man wasn't giving it to them.

One day I got a call at home from that same nice gentleman. He said, you are a very nice young man with a big career ahead of you. As a friend I want to help you by letting you know what happened to the last person who screwed with the price of gasoline. I don't know who did it but the poor guy ended up with two broken legs and still can't walk well to this day."

I got the picture. I told the corporation that for the minimal profit that a gas station could produce I did not think we should pursue the business and we didn't.

LIQUOR STORES

Within the first year with some help from others we designed and built a 4,000 square foot first class liquor store adjacent to the Turn*Style in Moline. The idea was to draw traffic with very competitive liquor prices and weekly advertised specials and make our money on selling wine, cheese, and barware. I hired Tom Quinn a former classmate from Cornell to run the first store, and a cheese expert, also from Cornell to be our cheese buyer and merchant.

Illinois did not have controls on liquor pricing but all of the surrounding states did. This store being on the border with Iowa we drew a lot of traffic from across the Mississippi. We even had a regular customer from Minneapolis who would call in his order in advance and drive down in a U-Haul truck to pick it up. He usually bought thousands of dollars worth on each trip. He claimed he bought for his whole community. If he was caught he would have lost the liquor and the truck and I don't know what else.

The store did well and we opened the next three stores in rapid succession. I was asked to leave Turn*Style and to focus my full attention on the liquor business. We set up "Case–n-Bottle" liquor stores in the corporate offices at O'Hare Plaza. In addition to the four liquor stores I had a liquor and wine buyer, a beer and bar accessories buyer, a cheese buyer and a store supervisor. We also negotiated all of the pricing with suppliers for Jewel Food Stores and Osco Drug Stores. Combined total we were doing about $50 million a year in alcoholic beverages.

I loved this business more than any I had experienced. This was an era when wine tastings became the rage and wine began to replace beer as the preferred drink for the younger set. The industry was loose, perhaps too loose with a lot of characters calling on us and a lot of gifts being offered.

Frequently I would arrive home from work and find several bottles or a case of something on my doorstep. Perhaps because of my father's early comment, "I've got him", or maybe because of my basic honesty, I never took a single one of the gifts. I took them all to the office and recorded them in a log book along with the disposition and what we were paid for the product.

A year later an ATF agent subpoenaed me and I testified with the help of a corporate lawyer. At the request of corporate I was given immunity which I did not need. I answered all of their questions and produced my diary for their inspection and the case was over. The agent issued a letter to Corporate indicating that I was completely exonerated from any wrong doing. Honesty pays.

There were a number of run-ins with what I might call the shady side of the industry. I was a member of the Board of Directors for the Illinois Retail Liquor Stores Association. We as a group decided that a law prohibiting the balancing of inventory between stores was unreasonably restrictive and for the benefit of the suppliers and drivers unions only. We decided to test the law with three different prominent chains breaking the law. The intention was not to be dishonest but to be caught and charged so that we could get this issue into court.

At the next meeting of the Board one of the test stores dropped off the board and out of the test. At the following meeting a second store dropped from the board and dropped the test. The remaining store owner blustered that he would see it through and he was disappointed that they were bullied out of the test case. At the very next meeting that fellow said he would no longer participate in the test. At coffee break I asked him privately what changed his mind. He said "Two well dressed Italian gentlemen visited him at his office and explained how much his family was going to miss him." I said what did you do? He replied "I pissed in my pants and said I wouldn't do it again."

Most businesses are clean but there are always elements to watch out for and to avoid at all cost.

As volume rose, Corporate Jewell became more interested in the liquor store business and began negotiations to buy Armanetti Liquors, a twenty one store chain in the Chicago area. Frank Armanetti was aging, his oldest son who was to take over the business was killed in a plane crash and his youngest son was thought to be incapable of running the operation. If Jewel bought his business my team and I would run it, his name would be preserved and he would be wealthy. For me this was the opportunity of a lifetime.

I visited every store, prepared a written review of each with a plan of action for it once we took over. This was exciting. Along with the stores were two bars which we would likely close. One of the provisions before the closing of the deal was that his business would stay clean.

Just before the deal was consummated two things happened. A large stockholder sent a letter of complaint to the Chairman that she did not think we should be in the liquor business. Of course we had been selling liquor in the food and drug stores for years but that didn't seem to bother her. More important, the front page of the Chicago Tribune reported that the feds were charging a number of tavern owners, one of which was Armanetti, with paying kick backs to Chicago Police officers. The deal was dead and so was corporate enthusiasm for our liquor stores.

A few days later Bill Lewis asked to meet with me. He proposed that I return to Turn*Style and explore and open some catalog showrooms which were the Wall Street rage at the time. I asked if it was a VP position and he said no. I told him I really liked the liquor business and I would have to think about it.

I mulled it over for a while and then called my father for his opinion. I told him of the offer and said I prefer the liquor business but I have great trust in Bill and Bill told me I should take his offer. I reasoned that Bill had never lied to me and I thought I should put my trust in him and take the job. Dad said you made the right decision. Bill had called him the night before and explained the opportunity and said when I called for his opinion not to let me make a mistake. I called Bill and accepted. Later that evening Bill called me and said I had been given the title of Vice President.

CATALOG SHOWROOMS

Once again I was investigating a new business. I had to know the products they sell, the pricing and margin structure, the inventory methods, the sale and retrieval process, and what if anything made them successful. My father taught me that you can't beat a man at his own business. There are always tricks of the trade that take time to learn. This was a good example. Good judgment would have been to take a long look and hire someone who was already experienced in the business rather than to start from scratch. Unfortunately, that just was not the Jewel way.

Catalog showrooms were a very hot topic on Wall Street and top corporate management wanted to get in on the action and perhaps boost the stock price. It was determined that this might be an addition to the Turn*Style business that might enhance their offering and improve their profits. In retrospect I think it was a diversion of our attention away from a very good business to which we needed to devote our full attention.

Fine jewelry was the largest profit contributor to the catalog showrooms. I had to hire a jeweler and work with him in New York buying millions of dollars worth of merchandise. I found an appliance store that was in an old bank building where the vault was still in the basement. I was able to rent the vault where a team could work to sort and price the merchandise until we were ready to open the stores.

We also needed to select all of the merchandise, negotiate pricing with the suppliers, photograph the merchandise and develop and print a catalog.

We opened four stores, all on the same day, in less than a year. They were called Turn*Style Plus reflecting their ties to the discount stores. We had a huge grand opening with Barbara Eden making an appearance at each store.

The Showrooms got off to a rough start with some of the systems not working properly and long delays for customers to get their products delivered. We should have taken more time for a shakedown period but the pressure was on to make headlines.

This was an enormous project at great expense. By the time we opened I think the bloom was already fading on Wall Street for catalog showrooms. It makes no sense at all to chase Wall Street. Be a leader or don't be anything.

Immediately I was asked to start on another project and the showrooms were turned over to someone else. They closed within a year or two. When one opens a new business it takes time to shake out the problems before it becomes successful. I have often thought that the definition of a real businessman is the one who turns failure into success. In this case Jewel corporate flitted from business to business and lost interest too quickly.

HYPERMARCHE

Here we go again. Bill was asked to put a team together to study the European Hypermarche type of retailing and then to introduce it to this country. He picked four guys, one of which was me, each specializing in one area or another. We first had to get an understanding of what these stores were all about. There was one in Montreal, Canada which Bill wanted us to visit first because it was close. Then we would go to Europe, a first for me.

The five of us flew to Montreal and had dinner in the hotel. Bill said look guys, we have a full day tomorrow and will be meeting with the top executives of this company so I want us all to go back to our rooms, get a good night's sleep and be up early tomorrow.

Not having been to Montreal I wasn't buying it. I waited about ten minutes in my room and then quietly slipped down to the elevator. As I exited the lobby to get a cab I ran into Bill. He said what are you doing? I replied I guess the same thing you're doing. He said let's get the Hell out of here before anyone sees us. We hit night spots until about 2:00 AM and then got a very short night's sleep. Bill and I became fast friends with each of us knowing we both liked to explore with a few, or more than a few, drinks so we made the rounds in lots of cities in lots of countries.

About this time Carolyn and I moved to Wheaton which was closer to the new office building. Debbie had been a cheerleader in her other school so this was a real let down for her. Karen and Laurie were scared about the move but I walked them around the block and stopped to introduce them to other children and soon they were well adjusted. Bill convinced me to join Medinah Country Club which we did and I loved it.

The whole group traveled all over Europe looking at stores. Hypermarche might literally be interpreted as huge market. It was basically everything under one roof in a store of 200 to 300 thousand square feet. Usually the stores had a tunnel like entrance which was almost claustrophobic which you walked through and then entered the store. We described the stores as having the "Oh my God" look. At the end of the entry tunnel one walked into a store with very high ceilings, with music blaring, and activity everywhere. Hucksters were shouting and selling everything. It was really an exciting environment.

In the produce department they were selling carrots by the fifty pound bag and the same with other vegetables. For wine you brought your own bottles and filled them up from a spigot on the wall. There was general merchandise, hardware, automotive, eye glasses, you name it and they had it.

On the perimeter there were restaurants and shoe repair shops etc. People came and spent the entire day having their meals when they needed a break. These stores did hundreds of millions of dollars in revenue each year.

Contrasting these stores with supermarkets in the United States we observed the following. Europe grew up under the feudal system with walled cities and lots of small shops to serve the needs of the people. There was no space to build our type of supermarket. Consumers in Europe were accustomed to storing vegetables in root cellars while we use refrigerators for small amounts at a time. Hypermarches were built way out in the country where land was cheap and there were no houses nearby. Our stores were built in highly populated areas on expensive tracts of land. Americans shop often for convenience while Europeans were willing to shop once a month making it a project. There were other differences too but these are some of the reasons why we could not duplicate their design.

When we returned from Europe we surveyed city after city in the U.S. to evaluate the competition, the road systems, traffic patterns, areas of population density etc. Unfortunately we estimated that the first store would cost about $20 million to get started. This was a big chunk of capital in the mid 1970s when business was soft and interest rates were high.

An amusing aside, each week we would leave town on Monday and return on Friday. On the way back we would all get partially oiled on the plane. Upon landing Bill would always say how about calling the brides and we'll go out to dinner. I would always say yes and the other guys would say no. I would call and of course Carolyn would say yes. One week Bill commented that Carolyn sure is flexible, she never has other plans. I said Bill you ask us every week so I tell her before I leave that we'll be going out to dinner with you on Friday.

Corporate decided that we could not afford that large a project at that time and that they would use parts of what we had learned in various types of our stores. Our group was disbanded with no assignments for about a month. That was really nerve racking. They couldn't figure out what to do with us but they didn't want to fire us. We went to "non-work" every day and looked for magazines to read to keep us busy. We were all worried that we would eventually be canned but we weren't.

REASSIGNED

A year or so prior to our reassignment Corporate again chased Wall Street which was then touting the Home Center industry. Jewel bought Republic Lumber which was a tiny company with two stores and a garage construction business. The only store really making money was very old with a very short remaining lease. A couple of new stores were built but were not producing a profit.

The garage construction division had been profitable but was soon exposed for bribing the building permit administrator for Chicago. In one case they had gotten a permit to build a garage right behind a telephone pole. The Republic salesman had convinced the owner that once the garage was built he could call the utility company and it would move the pole. The utility company just laughed and the owner had a garage that was not accessible. Both Stanley and Ira, the original owners, were discharged.

Corporate decided to consolidate the support operations for Osco Drug, Turn*Style and Republic Lumber. This meant purchasing, advertising, real estate; accounting, human resources etc would all be combined to form one "Merchandise Services Group". Key groupings within purchasing and advertising were developed and we were assigned to different ones. I was Vice President of purchasing for housewares, garden, patio, giftware, electronics, hardware, automotive and lumber and building materials.

In this capacity we selected the merchandise stores would carry, set pricing, developed the circular advertising strategy, and selected the products to be advertised and the pricing for those items. It is important to note that at the same time, and in the same market, we were developing competitive strategies for different categories of merchandise that might be a convenience product in the drug stores, a basic lead product in the home centers and a cut price product in the discount stores. We had to be very careful to match the product selection and the pricing to the marketing position of the chain. This in itself was an education.

There was a lot of favoritism in assigning people to key positions. All of the merchandise officers and general managers were to report to Bill Jacobs who was a former accountant with no personality. He knew absolutely nothing about merchandise or buying. Somewhere along the way he must have been told that winking when you are trying to convince some of something helps. He had developed a habit of winking constantly when he talked to anyone. We nicknamed him "Winkie".

Bill insisted on meeting with key vendors with the buyers and asked the dumbest questions. It was embarrassing for the buyers. Even the manufacturer's reps. made fun of him.

One time in an effort to build relationships with us he invited us all with our wives to his house for dinner. It was a big white house on a lot of property which we quickly dubbed "Tara". It was a buffet and at the end of the line was a large ham loaf covered with cherry sauce. We all assumed it was a cake for desert and that the meat would be passed at the table. Once we were all seated the hostess explained that we had missed the ham loaf and she sliced it and passed it around. One of the guys had pre-arranged with his sitter to call about the time we would be sitting down to dinner. He took the call, said he was sorry but their baby was sick and the sitter wanted them to come home, and left. He and his wife went out to dinner.

Morale was as low as it could get. We were over staffed and the top officers decided we were to reduce the buying staff from fifty four to twenty seven buyers. On what we called "Black Friday" we terminated twenty seven buyers and their secretaries. In a meeting conducted by the President of our merchandise services group, Dick Cline, he was asked if we could quickly get the empty desks out of the open area buying operation so that they would not depress the remaining people. He said "put a lily on them". What ever happened to merchants of empathy? Unfortunately this was indicative of the decline in people oriented leadership that was penetrating the company. Some people used to say that Dick Cline would kill his grandmother if it would help him get ahead.

I digress but think it is worth telling of another example of the deterioration of the merchants of empathy philosophy. Walt Elisha, a Harvard MBA and successful corporate trainee had risen to become President of Brigham's Ice Cream and Candy Shops. He began a program called TUK which was an acronym for Terminate Ugly Kids. He felt that no one wanted to buy ice cream from pimply faced teenagers so management would go around and make a list of the kids to fire. Can you imagine the lawsuits that would have arisen out of that had the program been revealed?

I received a call from a head hunter Jim Clovis, asking to meet with me. I was now at the point that I was ready to consider a change. I spent most of an afternoon with this gentleman but with him not revealing the name of his client. At the end of the interview he asked for a resume which I did not have but I prepared one over night. I also gave him a list of references.

I didn't hear from Jim for about two months but I did hear from some of the references. He apparently had some on the phone for more than an hour inquiring about me. That was encouraging.

Finally he called and said he wanted me to visit American Hardware Supply Company in Butler, Pennsylvania. I had never heard of the company or the town but I agreed to go. I went through very intense interviews the first day and on a second day I went to psychological testing.

There were no titles in this company but the head man was John Berryman, the general Manager. He called one evening and asked me to come back with Carolyn for him to make an offer and for her to see the community. In checking him out I had been warned by a supplier that he had a bankrupt character. Perhaps he did but he treated me well.

John explained that he planned to terminate the then Merchandise Manager in one year and that I would get that position if I did well during the year. I asked for a generous severance package which he refused saying that the Board of Directors would not allow him to write an employment contract. I told him that I would get a year of severance at Jewel and that I could not take this risk without protection. He finally said "well the Board didn't tell me I can't make an unemployment contract and he typed one out and gave it to me.

John prepared a letter that he and I were to keep in confidence stating that if I did well I would replace the head merchant in one year. He offered me $100,000 base pay and an opportunity to make multiples of that with short and long term bonuses. It was an offer I could not refuse.

Carolyn had been touring the city with a realtor all morning and came back at lunch time very unhappy. I went to John and said if we're going to make this deal work we have to get rid of the realtor and get someone to sell my wife on the community. He called in the head of human resources, Russ Thomas, and commanded him to make her like Butler. Russ spent the rest of the day with Carolyn and a better ambassador he could not have been. Russ and his wife are still our very close friends.

Debbie had spent the last year at the University of Kentucky. Like me she was not prepared for college and at the end of the year she joined the workforce. She opted not to relocate to Pennsylvania with us and remained in Chicago. Not long afterward she married Karl Kramer and they had one son, Justin the following spring.

During moving preparation Carolyn's father died suddenly in High Point, North Carolina. She and the kids flew down from Chicago as did I from Pennsylvania. The moving van was scheduled to arrive two days after the service so I returned without Carolyn to Wheaton. Carolyn never did return to Wheaton as she was helping her mother.

After cleaning the house Laurie and Karen and I started out by car for Pennsylvania. This was a wonderful opportunity for me to get into their heads. We had been a little concerned about the friends that Karen was hanging around with in Wheaton. Along the way I started asking them questions about what characteristics they thought were important in their selection of new friends. This was a really good discussion and it quickly became clear to me that I had gotten through to them.

In retrospect a lot of things went wrong with Jewel in the nine years that I worked there. Shortly after my departure both Turn*Style and Republic Lumber were sold. Republic Lumber was a waste to begin with as it was too small to support itself. Turn*style on the other hand was an outstanding discount store chain that resembled the Target stores of today. Corporate pushed Turn*Style management to expand geographically to Indianapolis and Grand Rapids before solidifying our home base in the Chicago area. K-Mart and others moved in and weakened our hold on that market.

While the corporate trainee program was superb training for future management I think they overloaded it with too many candidates. The result was a large number of candidates scrambling for fewer and fewer available positions as they rose higher and higher. Corporate recognized the log jam and began creating positions by thinning the top. It began to get around that if you were fifty years old you were over the hill and likely to be replaced. I for one wanted that to be my choice, not theirs.

Probably the biggest problem started right at the top. Chasing Wall Street for publicity and possible market valuation was poor judgment. One can't win the race by being a follower.

I was most fortunate to have been given so many different assignments and so much latitude to develop businesses as I saw fit. I guess one could say they made me a jack of all trades and master of none. This served me well as I move on because I had been trained to look for the idiosyncrasies of businesses and to act upon their differences.

CHAPTER XXIII

Lessons from the Jewel Experience

Leadership is more than directing or commanding other people. It is caring, communicating, participating, listening, and sharing.

The best corporate philosophy is only as good as the people who implement it.

Secure your primary market before reaching out to new markets.

If you are going to expand into new businesses hire experienced professionals in that field, be fully committed, and stay the course for enough years to become successful.

Overloading talent causes destructive infighting as high powered type "A" people scramble for the fewer and fewer top positions.

Don't chase Wall Street. Be the best at what you do. When you chase anything you are a follower rather than a leader.

Chapter XXIV

American Hardware Supply Company

In 1978 sales for American Hardware were $278 million. Our business was concentrated along the east coast of the United States. In the same business but generally focusing on different geographic areas were Cotter & Company (True Value Hardware Stores) and Ace Hardware, both in Chicago and Hardware Wholesalers Inc, (HWI) in Indiana. All four of us were cooperatives thereby rebating our profits as patronage dividends before taxes and paying no corporate income tax.

American Hardware Supply Company (AHS) was founded in 1910 in Pittsburgh, Pennsylvania. It was the first co-op in the hardware industry. The purpose of the founders was to eliminate the middle man commissions, consolidate purchasing for large volume commitments and better pricing, and to return all profits to the stockholders at the end of the year. Our company was capitalized by returning the profits at the end of the year to the stockholders (dealers) before taxes, partially in cash and the rest in stock. In the early days we served members in western Pennsylvania and Ohio and then through an acquisition expanded to Eastern Pennsylvania.

In the 1950s the company was saddled with a bad lease in Pittsburgh and at the same time was burdened by a bad union contract with the Teamsters. The then General Manager secretly sent a committee from the Board of Directors to find a new location in Butler County, about forty miles north of Pittsburgh. He found a way to break the lease and pushed us into a strike with the Teamsters at the same time. He smartly signed a new Teamster contract that gave them representation in Allegheny Country, our only facility at the time. He then announced that they were all fired because the company was closing the facility in Pittsburgh and relocating to Butler County which was not included in the contract.

Butler was loaded with farm boys who knew how to work. He trained them to drive semis by driving through town. He vowed to pay higher than union scale and to have open communication with all employees on a regular basis. There would be no third party interfering with our management and employee relationships. He did escape the union but the case was tested all the way to the Supreme Court which fortunately decided in our favor because the union had accepted severance pay. Companies can no longer run away from unions in this manner.

Serving independent hardware stores was a joy. Generally speaking they were family owned operations which passed from father to son through the generations.

They were grateful for the support that we gave to them. There was no requirement for them to purchase their merchandise from us but we were usually the lowest priced supplier on all products. The annual rebate somewhat clouded the issue because it was calculated on each item and could be large or small depending on the mark-up for the item. There really was no way for the hardware dealer to calculate the final cost of an item after rebate. Business was done largely on trust in the philosophy of the business.

We were a complete resource for the stores. Once they bought stock in our company they were entitled to all of our services. They could buy through our warehouse, or have their orders pooled with other dealers and delivered through a processing center upon arrival or through drop shipment directly from the manufacturer to their store with billing to us. We guaranteed the credit of all of our members which gave the small store power with the manufacturer but also required us to have a strong credit department to watch over the stores. Conversely with us guaranteeing the credit of the stores the manufacturers saved money in their credit departments by only having to watch us, not hundreds of small stores. The manufacturers in return reduced our prices by what they called functional rebates.

We found store locations for desirous investors, designed and built the stores, stocked the merchandise, trained the owner, prepared the advertising, handled his accounting if he so desired, implemented his computer program which was designed and owned by us, helped with his marketing strategies, taught him how to turn his business over to his son or daughter, and taught the kids how to take over the business from their parents with as little tension as possible. We did everything just like a franchisor but we were a dealer owned business, not a franchise, the difference being the tax exempt status.

Store owners were grateful for our leadership. I recall one local meeting wherein I was asking the members to invest heavily in an advertising program that we wanted to run. I was getting serious resistance until one man stood up and said "I don't like what you are asking us to do but you made me rich and I owe it to you to give you my support". What a great feeling that gave me.

Our Board of Directors was made up of store owners. They were elected by the membership and served three year terms. One third was up for reelection each year. There was no restriction on how many terms a person could serve. The Board was generally supportive of management's direction, in fact, sometimes too supportive. There were a few outspoken challengers but only on rare occasions did they get aggressive. There were only two chairmen during my tenure with American Hardware which was renamed ServiStar shortly after I joined the company. The first one was a wonderful guy but he was too old for the job. He went along with the General Manager without much question and frankly dozed off and on during the Board meetings.

The second Chairman was more involved, quite strong in his thinking and planning but much too highly political. Whatever he did was to enhance his own position. Strong support of the President (Titles changed in my third year.) strengthened his own position; however, as soon as my predecessor and I retired he discarded allegiance and put us in the trash can.

Most Directors were the salt of the earth. One in particular, Jay Feinsod was a progressive retailer with several successful stores. He was more of a thinker and a quiet questioner and peacemaker. He quietly helped to steer the company.

JOHN BERRYMAN

John recruited me and was General Manager at the time that I joined the company. John was one of the most unusual men that I have ever met. One time after he had told me some of the extraordinary things he had done for employees whose spouses were dieing of cancer I made the mistake of complementing him on caring so much for people. He strongly said "Don't ever make that mistake again. I only help people because it is good for the business and for no other reason." He had an ego beyond belief. He professed that he had read the entire set of encyclopedias while shaving by making a stand for the books to perch upon while he shaved. He was a science fiction writer in his spare time under a pen name. He was an outstanding orator and had what I would call the "Jim Jones charisma". In meetings with prospective members he often goaded people into asking him how much he was paid and was happy to blurt it out the answer. When someone would ask how he could justify that much pay when the heads of the other co-ops were paid so much less he would say "They know what they are worth".

John had been married multiple times and was not shy about his conquests. At Christmas he often had all of management and their spouses to his house for cocktails before the annual company Christmas party. He would invite everyone to tour his house. In the master bedroom over his bed was a large painting of his secretary. Now what kind of message does that send to the staff?

John had made that agreement with me that I would replace my boss Jim Marone in one year if I did well. About two months after I arrived Jim asked me to write the five year plan with organization charts etc. John was out of town so I could not ask his advice. I completed the task having removed Jim in the second year. I was not going to put on paper anything that might indicate that I would accept less that the commitment that had been made to me. When Jim saw the report he turned purple he was so mad. He commanded me to take it back and put him back in the organization. I apologized and said he had mentioned he would be retiring down the road but he had not been specific so I just made an assumption. I knew that my lame answer didn't fly.

When John returned I told him what had happened. He chomped on his cigar and said "Son you've really got balls". He had a good laugh.

John had also told me that I would be a candidate to replace him if he stayed long enough for me to get some experience. Unfortunately John had a heart attack in the spring and never came back.

In the confusing days after the heart attack we were waiting for the Board to announce some leadership direction. Into my office walked Larry Zehfuss, the finance officer, who said he was going to be taking John's place at least until they see if he would ever come back. He said tell me what your deal is with John. I said I do have an agreement with John but he swore me to secrecy and I can't share it with you without his approval. Larry fumed and insisted that I give him what he wanted. I said if you have the authority that you claim then you'll find John's copy in his files. Otherwise I can't help you. That was my first but not my last difficult encounter with Larry.

He came back the next day and said I read the letter but I don't know what I am going to do. He didn't want to change the management team if he was just taking over. I said the letter is quite clear and I believe my performance meets the standards set for me. I expect to have Jim's job in July. He walked out. July first Jim was moved over to advertising and I was given his job. Sometimes one must be committed to a course of action and push his luck.

LARRY ZEHFUSS

Larry took over with enthusiasm. Within the first year or two he changed the name of the company to ServiStar. This had been in the works for some time and had been tested in Rochester, New York, which was a classic test market city. He also upgraded our titles to the more standard President and Vice President.

Larry was a CPA by background and had been the CFO for AHS for several years. He was somewhat insecure in his job and would not permit his officers to socialize together. Once when we had formed a bridge group of four couples he called in one officer and said he would fire him if he didn't drop out of the bridge group. He claimed there would be too much communication between the four of us which was unfair to the other officers, mainly himself.

On another occasion when one of the officer's sons got married and Larry could not be at the wedding he grilled our HR VP about the event. He even asked who he danced with. When he found out that he had danced with my wife Carolyn he said he would fire him if he ever did that again. He accused him of buttering me up because he thought I might become President.

Larry did a lot of good things too. He was always reading about new ways of motivating employees and maximizing productivity. He tried many of them which was an education for all of us even though most of the new philosophies worked better in books than they did in practice,

He managed our finances well and compensated us well. It should be noted that one reason for the very high pay for our officers was that as a cooperative we did not have access to any stock options. If we were to recruit top talent we had to offset the options that publicly traded companies had. He managed the Board well also and got some special health insurance programs for our retirement that were very generous. He was also out in front of the industry at all of the functions and helped to keep our reputation in good stead.

One of his unusual quirks was to divide and conquer his officers. At annual review time he would grade you and say things like some of the officers say this about you. One would never know if he made it up or if one of your fellow officers was trying to undermine you. It was a horrible way to manage people. There was little or no defense for such blind accusations. It caused the officers neither to trust nor to confide in each other

As the years went by Larry's ego grew. At one point he ran a contest for the company to guess the sales for the month. The prize was a ride around the parking lot in his new car. Ego is a serious disease of top executives. One must do everything in his power to fight it off. When I became President I asked one of my officers to tell me if he thought I was catching the ego disease. I meant it but he probably would have been uneasy telling me something like that.

When I was in the transition period to become President, Larry spent months at his home in Colorado which we referred to as the Western White House. We would hear nothing from him until one day he would come in and without saying anything to me he would rescind job postings or other decisions I had made. He totally undermined my authority and without any conversation to find out why I made the decisions that I did. It was a very hard time. I felt that I had to read every piece of information and to be better informed than he was. I worked late every night and all day on Saturdays and Sundays.

At one point Larry got into a snit with Butler Country Club and ordered us not to entertain there any longer. He was going to try to punish the club financially. He said to me and to one other officer that he and the two of us should pick country clubs in the Pittsburgh area and the company would pay for the memberships. At a Board meeting toward the end of my transition a Director asked Larry if any officers had country club memberships that were paid for by the company. Larry lied and said no. The next day I was traveling with the Chairman and I said needed to confide in him. I said Larry had made a mistake about the club memberships and that I did not want the Board to ever think that I heard his statement and covered it up. The Chairman kept it quiet until Larry retired and then had the company bill him for the price of the membership. He excused the two of us because we had been told to buy the memberships by Larry.

Also when Larry retired our CFO told the Board that he had been ordered to load negative equity into our subsidiary Speer Hardware and to upload false profits to the parent corporation. The Board was furious and rightfully so.

COMPETITION

With the thousands of hardware stores in the United States it was easy to grow until the mid-eighties. Fewer sons and daughters of hardware store owners were inclined to want to spend the hours necessary to run a retail business. On top of that, the parents generally wanted to turn the business over to the kids but considered it their retirement account and wanted some income from the ongoing business. Often there wasn't enough profit to provide retirement for the parents and a good lifestyle for the son or daughter and their families. Also too often the parents had multiple children and tried to keep everyone in the business so as not to show favoritism and therefore all of them had too little money.

Increased competition from Wal-Mart and Home Depot and Lowe's also drove a lot of stores out of business. The results were a declining population of stores and higher incursion into each other's markets by the four cooperatives with aggressive efforts to steal each others members. The 80s and 90's were decades of intense competition with the other cooperatives. At the same time we knew we had to teach our stores how to survive the entry of the "Big Box" stores into their markets.

In the early 80's we strategized that we should take advantage of our strengths and broaden our base of stores into other fields. We were good at warehousing and distribution and we knew how to run a co-operative. We could reach into other areas such as the rental business, or garden centers, or industrial supply stores to provide greater volume and more stability in the event of a downturn in one or another sector.

We also started our movement west with the opening of a new warehouse in Charleston, Illinois, right in the heart of the markets of Ace and True Value. The war had started.

STRATEGIC DIRECTION

As an officer group we agreed that we needed to find ways in which our members could defend themselves against the "Big Box" stores. With Larry's approval I introduced a junior officer but very bright young lady, Joan Trach to my former professor and advisor, Dr. Wendell Earle. He had taught me that in the early part of the century the independent grocery stores were being run out of business by the introduction of chain supermarkets. The independent stores regained their strength in the 60s. The situation was so much like ours that I asked Joan to go to Ithaca and ask Dr. Earle what made the difference.

Quite simply, the independent stores formed cooperatives to supply them at more competitive prices, and they built strong relationships with the local community which chain stores had trouble doing. Chain management frequently moves from store to store which effectively prevents building a local relationship. Also, the profits of chain stores leave the community for corporate funds while the profits of the independent retailer remain within the community.

With the help of Marc Advertising of Pittsburgh we developed a cause marketing program around vocational education called "Tools for Tomorrow". Conceptually, the vocational students would be more likely to be our future customers than would other students. It was also true that these students were under appreciated and less likely to receive any kind of scholarship funding. With the help of Marc Advertising and Vocational and Industrial Clubs of America (VICA) we launched a terrific program of scholarships through our stores and began a variety of community projects utilizing the students at out stores.

In my opinion this program had the potential to be similar to Ronald McDonald and could strengthen the business of our members as well as to align them more closely with our business. It was a bitter disappointment that my successor allowed this program to die after my retirement. Perhaps it was through financial necessity or it may have been because his education was in finance rather than marketing. I think it was a terrible mistake.

We also set out to develop specific strategies that our members could use to compete more effectively with Home Depot and other box stores. Don Belt, SVP Marketing, Gene O'Donnell, SVP Merchandise, and I called a meeting of all of our stores in Atlanta where Home Depot had started roughly ten years earlier. We spent an entire afternoon asking what categories were most affected by the new competition, how did this change one year after they opened, how did the prices compare in the beginning and a year later, which categories were not affected, what did their customers like and dislike about the new store etc. We did this progressively in the newer markets chronologically to determine how their strategies changed over the years. We learned a lot. I won't go into detail other than to say that we developed an effective competitive strategy that helped to save many members' businesses. Don wrote a "How to Compete with Home Depot" book that we shared with members who faced that competition.

We also tried television advertising but never could spend enough to build the gross rating points sufficiently to move products off the store's shelves or to increase our consumer recognition ratings. We found that print media was more effective for our products and for our consumer base.

COAST TO COAST STORES

In about 1989 Coast to Coast stores which was headquartered in Denver and had two warehouses on the west coast ran into financial trouble. They were owned by a larger corporation that wanted to dispose of that entity. For us it could be an avenue to the west coast giving us warehouse support so that we could begin to sign stores that far away from our closest warehouse which was in Illinois.

Through negotiations Larry struck a deal in which Coast to Coast would remain a separate entity but we would purchase the warehouses, the computer system and other assets giving them an opportunity to continue to function independently without the overhead that had been such a burden to them. It was good for both organizations if we could stick to the plan. We would use the warehouses and some of the office space and they would operate separately with less overhead.

Unfortunately as time went on the management of Coast to Coast began to feel their oats and wanted to seek independence from us. We had two separate Boards of Directors and one interlocking Board covering the joint entity. On the day that I took over as President I was asked to give my opinion of the future of the relationship with Coast to Coast. I stated that eventually we were going to have to merge the two organizations for significant administrative savings. This being the last meeting ServiStar Board meeting that Larry would attend he immediately warned the Board to be ready for a fight with the Coast Board. He then went to his office and informed the Coast Board by e-mail of my comments. The only justification for his disclosure of confidential board information was that he wanted me to fail. The shit hit the fan.

Needless to say, I was always at odds with the Coast Directors and their top management. It became clear through bankers and other suppliers that the President of Coast to Coast was looking for financing to escape our grip and to reestablish themselves on their own. We had invested a lot of our dealer's money in Coast to Coast so separation or a spin off was not an acceptable option for us.

Through a number of secret meetings with our Board and consultants and a cadre of attorneys we established a plan for our own decisive takeover.

We called our annual meeting of both boards and all officers for a weekend in Portland at a hotel. This kept everyone away from the phones. Cell phones were not an issue at that time.

During the meeting the directors asked the officers to recess to a conference room for some special instructions and training by our HR VP, Russ Thomas. I was asked by the ServiStar Chairman to remain which was protested by the Coast Board but to no avail.

Through some fine print in our agreement our Board was able to make a motion to add me to the Board. That was protested by the Coast Board but they could not stop it. This gave the ServiStar side a majority.

Then a motion was made to fire the President of Coast to Coast. Our majority carried. Through a series of motions we took over the business. Their Board started to walk out but they were told that we had a full plan of action and they would be wise to hear it through before they left. One of their Directors threw up under the pressure.

While all of this was going on we had the customer service representatives from ServiStar come in on Saturday and telephone all Coast and ServiStar sales reps to instruct them to be in Denver in the morning for a meeting. Of course none of the officers could be reached because they were secluded with us.

We recessed for a few minutes and I went to the meeting room of officers and asked to see the Coast President. Russ quietly followed me out of the room to a private room where we terminated the President. At first he refused to believe it could be done but he was forced to take a severance contract with him to consider.

The next morning we met in Denver and laid out a plan for Coast dealer meetings in each large metropolitan area. We forced Coast officers to travel with ServiStar officers so that we could control the meetings and so that they could not get together to develop a retaliatory campaign.

The Coast store owners were furious even though we stated that together we would be able to save them money. We had a real fight on our hands. Early in the week I called the President of their paint supplier, one of the most important lines and highest volume lines of any hardware store. ServiStar owned its own paint manufacturing plant which had excess capacity and could easily take over the Coast business. I told their supplier that I would guarantee to leave the paint business with him for three years if he would insure me that his sales force would speak positively of our forced merger and if he would grant an immediate ten percent reduction in the price of paint for all stores. He agreed and I immediately put out a bulletin to all stores announcing the new pricing that we had negotiated. This gave us credibility and eliminated most of the fight. Money talks!

BECOMING PRESIDENT

As Larry approached retirement (55) the Board hired an outside consultant to determine who should be his successor. He interviewed all officers and junior officers to evaluate and to seek opinions and to get a feel for reputations. In 1990 Larry took me by surprise and told me that the Board had asked him to offer me the Presidency after a two year transition period. He encouraged me to consider it carefully as it was a real challenge. I knew he wanted me to turn it down.

Of course I accepted and as I mentioned earlier I drove myself to be on top of everything. I probably worked seventy five to eighty hours per week for two years. When I did take a vacation Larry would call me back for nothing. When we went to Colorado Springs for industry golf he sent me back the next morning to handle some situation that could have been handled over the phone. He made my life miserable. At one point he told me to fire a perfectly good man that I had hired several years before. When I argued he said either you do it or I will do it and he won't be treated as well if I do it". I really cared for the guy but I had no choice. He never forgave me. Larry was just testing me. He would like to have told the Board that I didn't have the guts to terminate someone.

In his last ServiStar Board meeting wherein we determined annual bonuses and compensation he said to the Board "I know this will sound like I am taking all of the goodies but I am only looking out for the company. No one should get a bonus this year except me because the profits are not there. Also, all company cars should be eliminated and the special medical plans for retirement should be cancelled for future retirees after me." He went on "my bonus should be paid since this is the last one that I would get and we would have no opportunity to make up for passing on this year." Fortunately I had done my homework better than Larry and showed the Board where the funds would come from and what the profit picture would be. I certainly didn't want to begin my Presidency by telling all of the officers that they would not get bonuses and to turn in their company cars. We kept the cars and the insurance programs and got the bonuses.

I later learned that just before Larry's retirement he went to Pete, the Chairman, and asked to stay on as President saying that he would fire me and eventually recruit someone from outside the business to replace him. Pete told him that the Board had made up their mind and that they were going to support me as the President.

One day my secretary called me crying and stated that Larry's former secretary told her that she should not get comfortable in her job because there was a secret arrangement between Larry and the Board that after a few months I would be fired and Larry would come back to run the company. I called Pete and he flatly denied it. Whatever he said, it was still unsettling.

Shortly after I became president one of my officers asked me if I was aware of a number of letters Larry had been sending to Pete criticizing my performance and undermining my position. He said that Larry had shown them to another officer on Larry's home computer. It is one thing to share opinions with the Chairman but to plant seeds of doubt with my subordinates is dirty play. Again, I called Pete and asked about the letters to which he wanted to know where I had heard about them. He then called Larry and asked if he had shown copies of the letters to this particular officer. Larry lied and denied it. When Pete told him he knew that he had shown them to the officer on his home computer Larry had no choice but to admit it. At that point Pete had our attorney draw up a letter to Larry advising that all communication with company personnel and undermining of my position had to stop or he would discontinue some of Larry's retirement benefits.

At our first Board meeting after Larry's departure I told the Board that I would stay for five years. My wife had Multiple Sclerosis and I wanted to retire before she became too immobilized so that we would have some time to enjoy life together. I further explained that there were a lot of corrections that had to be made that would put a temporary strain on profits. I asked the Board to set up a future bonus payout once we had corrected our problems. This would benefit the other officers but not me.

Our CFO advised the Board that many things had been capitalized that should not have been such as truck expenses for delivery to experimental markets like Canada or the west coast. He also said that Speer

Hardware, a subsidiary had at Larry's instruction built up negative equity so that false profits could be transferred up to the parent corporation. This was devastating to the Board but at least we now had things out in the open and could deal with them.

I asked the Board to accept some years of lower earnings as I took down the negative equity and worked off the capitalized items. I said I would clean up the finances and then I would merge us with True Value in a period of five years. They gave me their support and I did it.

TRUE VALUE

After careful analysis of the different cooperatives I concluded that True Value had similar standards and ethics to those of ServiStar. True Value seemed to be the right target for a merger.

For several years there had been interest expressed by the four cooperatives to try to do some things together. After Larry's retirement I received calls asking that we try to get together. I was told that the other presidents were not comfortable with Larry and that is why nothing had developed in the past.

We started a group called ACHS, an acronym for the four of us. We met regularly under the sharp scrutiny of a lawyer to see that we did not discuss anything that would put us in jeopardy. We considered manufacturing together and importing together and actually did some backhauling for each other. Overall it was not a very successful effort.

I called Dan Cotter, President of Cotter & Company, True Value Stores, and suggested we get together for a private discussion. He agreed and said to meet him in a private conference at the American Airlines lounge at O'Hare Airport on a particular day.

At the meeting I told Dan that together we had twenty three warehouses and together we could probably survive with fourteen. I said it is costing more that $2.00 per mile to drive a truck and we are both going many miles to towns that have both of our stores. We could save tremendously by putting both deliveries on one truck. I talked about the overhead that we could eliminate through a merger and the fact that we could combine our paint production into one plant as we both owned our own manufacturing facilities. I stipulated that I would only merge with him if he agreed that this was only the first step and that we should target the other cooperatives down the road.

Dan was agreeable and suggested that we take a week and each of us put together a list of potential deal breakers and get back together to see if we might have a match. We did and we found nothing that appeared to be insurmountable.

We each put together a team of four people to begin the planning and the negotiations. Purposely Dan and I stayed out of the face to face negotiations so that we would never be put in a position from which we could not back down. We had selected a secret meeting place in Cleveland for the two teams of negotiators to meet. When an impasse occurred Dan and I would be called and we would coach from the background. The discussions went on for weeks because they not only involved the agreement but also the future structure and plans for blending the organizations including the officer structure. This was a really sensitive area as they were talking about their own jobs.

During December, 1996 the two Boards met together in Pittsburgh and agreed to the merger. The Cotter Chairman had confided in Pete that I could have any position I wanted, that I should not let this opportunity pass us by. I had great respect for Dan Cotter, the president of Cotter & Company and felt that he was critical to achieving a positive vote from the True Value Stores. I told Dan that I would be happy to be the President, COO of the new company and he could be the CEO as long as the staff reported to me and I controlled the day to day activities. He agreed.

After a year we both announced our planned retirements and a change in structure so that we were Co-CEOs for the final year. A successor for both of us was named. Part of the deal I had made with Dan was that I would retire first but that he had to retire within one year of my retirement so that the next high ranking ServiStar Officer could take over as president. I wanted our stores to be strongly represented as the organization went through the digestion of the merger.

The year that I retired our volume peaked at $4.328 billion. That is almost sixteen times what it was when I joined the company. Much of the growth came from acquisitions and mergers but growth of any kind is still growth.

I retired at the end of 1998 and Dan at the end of 1999. Unfortunately in either 2000 or 2001 some accounting irregularities were discovered that had originated in Cotter & Co. and had festered for many years resulting in a temporarily unexplained loss of about $120 million. How this irregularity was not discovered during due diligence I will never know. It would have killed the merger. This loss nearly toppled the entire company. My successor was forced out by the lending institutions, some portions of the business were sold off to raise capital, fingers were pointed in every direction etc. After a thorough investigation it was concluded that the errors were the fault of the Cotter CFO who through unintentional bad judgment made some accounting errors in the way that he tracked inventory which, over years, caused the entire mess.

CHAPTER XXV

Lessons Learned

The most important tool that a leader has is communication. It is impossible to satisfy the insatiable curiosity of employees, staff, shareholders, and Board members. To be an effective leader one must anticipate what interested parties want to know and either preempt their questions or be prepared to respond to their questions with confidence and conviction in an appropriate forum. Regardless, there will always be complaints of insufficient communication.

Many high ranking executives continue to attend industry and corporate functions years after retirement. I watched several of them attend our markets or the annual golf events at the Broadmoor only to find that their jokes are no longer as funny, they are not in as high demand for foursome tee times, they are no longer on the dinner invitation list. It is a rude and sad awakening when one comes to the realization that their popularity was more a result of their power than their personality. I felt sorry for them and committed to myself that when I retire, I will not look back, nor will I continue to attend industry functions.

Ego is an insidious cancer that is spawned by power and authority. It is impossible to not be self satisfied when thousands of people applaud your presence at markets and meetings. Somehow one needs to come to grips with reality. As they say, "you put your pants on the same way as everyone else, one leg at a time". One must recognize that the success of the corporation is more dependent upon the efforts of the lowest levels of production than it is on top management.

Greed is another disease of the high ranking executive. It is so easy to justify anything by saying "I earned it". Or perhaps to say no one will ever know. I gave some examples in earlier chapters but there are unfortunately too many more that could be mentioned. The facts are that someone will know. For high ranking people there is always someone watching and judging. A good rule of thumb is to ask yourself what my children or grandchildren would think.

Life, whether it be business or personal is one mass of varying opinions. It is discussions, arguments, negotiations, strategic thinking, the selling of ideas etc. One can not address issues unless one listens to what they are. To be effective one must understand the issues and do enough homework to recognize the varying points of view. It is never harmful to accept the point of view of others if you can see that they are more correct than you are.

Surround yourself with people who are willing to disagree with you. If everyone agrees with you all of the time there is no need for everyone else. One time

I told an associate that he agrees with me too much. I said someday I am gong to intentionally say something dumb and if you agree with me I will know that I don't need you. I guarantee you that he weighed our conversations more carefully after that.

Nobody is an expert in everything. Real leaders employ experts in whom they have great trust. They each should know more about their specialty than you do. Your job is to listen to their advice, evaluate it, piece it together with the advice of others and then make the decisions. Once the decisions are made they are yours to live with, not theirs.

Chapter XXVI

Retirement

In February following my retirement, the Board of directors surprised me with a retirement party in California to which they had brought our children and grandchildren. They had also arranged for a photographer to take a family portrait in the hotel garden and to give us a large framed copy for our wall in Florida where it hangs today. What a nice gift.

Also from my associate officers I was given cooking lessons at a school at the Ritz Carlton near Jacksonville, Florida. Another thoughtful gift as cooking is one of my many hobbies.

Contrary to what some younger people think, retirement is not a pasture where one wiles away their years until the grim reaper gets him. It is an exciting opportunity to solidify friendships, to make new friends, and to devote time to the many interests one has. If you have no interests or hobbies it can be a boring time. But for that matter, if you have no interests you're boring too.

When I first retired a fellow retiree said "retirement is great, you get up in the morning with nothing to do and when you go to bed at night you've only done half of it". He is so right. There is no time for boredom. I really don't know how I ever had time to work for a living.

As I approached retirement Carolyn and I put a lot of thought into where we would like to spend the rest of our lives. I encourage everyone to devote a lot of time to this as it will be one of the most important decisions you will make. With luck you will have a lot of years of good health to spend with people and an environment that meet your needs.

For us, we reasoned that eventually we would want only one place and not to migrate from winter to summer homes. That ruled out the desert southwest. We like seawater so Florida was a natural. With Carolyn's MS condition the turbulence of the Atlantic waves was not acceptable so the calmness of the Gulf became our target. Having honeymooned in Naples the decision was easily made.

Important to us was a club environment with easy access to golf and a small enough membership so that we would eventually know nearly everyone. It is nice to walk into the lounge or the dining room and to be able to greet everyone. We also wanted to have a bridge club to help Carolyn in her introduction to the membership. I could meet people through golf but with her restrictions she needed other avenues.

We researched the communities for at least a year, measured them against a list of criteria which we had developed and made our choice. We selected a lot, a builder, an architect, an interior designer, and planned a home that was fully accessible for Carolyn and designed for good socializing and relaxation. We could not be more pleased with our selection and decisions.

Early in retirement I did a little consulting and was on one or two boards. It was not something I enjoyed. I also have done some guest lecturing at Edison College which I find more enjoyable. While preparing remarks for a lecture it occurred to me that a career such as mine is like a pinball game. The bachelor's degree is like the plunger that launches you into the world of opportunities. The effort that went into studies may determine the power of the launch. Like the pinball that bounces off of scoring opportunities the candidate is exposed to job opportunities or decisions. Sometimes one drops straight through with little point count. Others hit the flippers and bound upward to new opportunities. The key in a career just like in pinball is to know when and how hard to hit the flipper.

Golf and bridge occupy the largest portion of my free time. I play golf in the winter at least four times per week and we play duplicate bridge on Monday and couple's bridge several other times each week. Occasionally I fish either in the local ponds where there are huge bass or with a guide in the waters of the Ten Thousand Islands.

When the opportunity arises we visit the children and grandchildren or they visit us. We have also found cruises with friends to be a great way to travel even though they are tough on the diet.

After reading an article about a local Multiple Sclerosis Charity I felt that I should get involved and give back to the community. I had lunch with the founders and they offered me a position on the board. Since then I have risen to chairman and have led the organization for the past five years. Our mission is to improve the quality of life for those in Southwest Florida who are afflicted with Multiple Sclerosis. This takes about twenty hours per week.

Suffice it to say that retirement is wonderful if you have a variety of interests to keep your attention.

Chapter XXVII

Multiple Sclerosis

While seeing our family physician in 1983 I inquired about what type of doctor Carolyn should see because she seemed to have a pinched nerve in her back. He asked about the symptoms and I said after walking short distances she begins to drag her left foot. He insisted that I call her from his office and make an appointment for her for the next day.

When I came home from work the next day Carolyn said to call Dr. Nunna, he wanted to talk to me. Dr. Nunna said I'm sorry to tell you this but your wife has cancer of the spine. He wanted me to check her into the local hospital the next morning. I questioned his judgment to which he said trust me, I know. If we are going to save your wife we need to act quickly. We need to find a place to send her and the best doctors because this is something we can not handle at our hospital.

Because the next day was Karen's high school graduation Carolyn delayed her hospital stay by one day. Dr. Nunna brought in a specialist from Pittsburgh who confirmed his diagnosis. After a couple of days of extremely unpleasant testing Dr. Nunna advised me that he was wrong. He apologized for such strong actions but said that if it had been cancer we would have needed very quick action. He then said that it was either Multiple Sclerosis or Lou Gehrig's Disease and he suspected she was a little old for MS to be showing up for the first time. He said he had sent a spinal tap to Atlanta for a more specific diagnosis. Shortly afterward the neurologist from Pittsburgh said that even though they did not find the cancer it is still there and if we were to have any chance to save Carolyn that I must get her to a major facility such as the Mayo Clinic or the Cleveland Clinic

I then took Carolyn to the Cleveland Clinic where a Dr. Furlan said "if I didn't know better I would say that your wife has cancer of the spine but I do know better. She has Multiple Sclerosis." "There are no treatments and the disease will take a variety of courses that are totally unpredictable. I'll be your doctor of record so call me whenever you want to." I asked why I would want to call him and he answered I don't know but you will.

Not knowing much about MS our family handled the news as well as could be expected. Fortunately we were both inclined to be open and to talk about the situation. We did a lot of reading of text books and medical journal articles to become better informed and to brace ourselves for what to expect. Carolyn joined the National MS Society but went to only one meeting which she found to be too upsetting because of all of the severely afflicted people who attended.

A letter of sympathy from my aunt was very troubling to her because my aunt commented about people she knew who had MS and how their husbands had left them. This on top of reading that more than 80% of marriages of MS patients end in divorce left her depressed and fearful.

People reacted in a variety of ways. Some shied away, not knowing what to say. Some bent over backward to do things with Carolyn to help keep her busy. Some talked openly with us about the disease and others didn't mention it.

Our lifestyle had changed quickly. Couples tennis and golf were over. The consequence of this was that some of our regular social activities ended. This was hard to take for both of us. In the spring when people came outdoors to work on the lawn or in the garden she could no longer participate. Small things like the conversations about what had been planted that day were troubling.

Carolyn was rightfully depressed which concerned me greatly. When at our market in Baltimore I returned to the hotel room frequently to check on her well being. One day when we had a long drive for just the two of us I addressed the possibility of suicide directly and she assured me that she would not do that to our children or to me. I had worried for no good reason, just recognition of the degree of depression.

On another occasion I addressed her attitude as frankly as I could. I said that "if you have good spirits people will want to be around you but if you don't they will avoid you. I also said that I can deal with the extra work the disease puts on me, I can handle the change in social functions, I can deal with the lifestyle changes but I can't deal with a bad attitude. I have a deeply stressful job that I need to do well in order to support our family. A bad attitude will detract from my performance and the quality of our marriage so please concentrate on having a good attitude for me. I'll do the rest". She did and still does to this day.

It occurred to me that MS is a family disease, not just the disease of the individual. Of course the disabling impact is to only one person but the rest of the family is also impacted by the necessary care and lifestyle changes. I came to the reality that a spouse can walk away from the disease and resume life as it was with someone else or can remain committed to the vows we had made years before. I chose to play the hand I was dealt and I am glad that I did.

Often we hear of couples wherein the caregiver walked away from the patient. While they are criticized by many I refuse to do that. I have seen too many cases where the fault lies with the patient's failure to accept the illness and to make the best of a difficult situation.

Carolyn's illness fortunately has progressed slowly and she was still walking with a cane, fifteen years after diagnosis and at the time of my retirement. Now she is confined to a wheelchair but we play bridge, entertain, travel, etc. This bump in the road may have slowed us down but it didn't knock the wheel off the car.

Chapter XXVIII

Travels

Carolyn and I had the good fortune to travel extensively while with ServiStar. The company had annual dealer trips to interesting places as well as reward trips for volume increases. We hosted many of the trips particularly after I became President.

We spent time in many Asian countries including Russia, Thailand, Singapore, Hong Kong, Korea, Taiwan and Japan. We also covered most of Europe with hardware dealers who we enjoyed thoroughly. On all trips we had trained guides to educate us. All of these trips were professionally planned. I kept copious notes on my tape recorder every night which were transcribed by my secretary upon return. We now have a fine record of all of our travels.

One of our best trips that was not business related was to tour Europe with Bill & Jo Lewis our continuing close friends from my time at Jewel. We flew to Switzerland, rented a van, and drove through Switzerland, Lichtenstein, Austria, Germany and

France. None of us could speak a foreign language, nor did we know the international road signs, but we survived, had a lot of laughs and some fine food.

We enjoyed many vacations with Bill and Jo as well as other friends who joined us. The four of us frequently went to Acapulco with two other couples where we rented a home with a staff. The guys played golf in the mornings. The rest of the days were filled with activities from bull fights to sport fishing.

We did the same for four or five years with Bill and Jo in Jamaica at a resort called Tryall. A variety of couples joined us over the years. Again we had a private home with a full staff. The first year we rented a car and drove all over the island but after that we hired a driver which was much safer. I recall going to Negril Beach for a picnic to find out that most of the sun bathers were nude. Not us!

Our daily routine was for the men to play golf early. We would meet the ladies at the bar by the ocean when we were done with golf and have a few bloody marys. Then we would return to the house for lunch, and then an afternoon of swimming and bridge. In the evening it was cocktails and dinner and then a game of trivial pursuit accompanied by generous amounts of black Russians.

Since retiring we have taken to cruises for our touring as we can avoid the unpacking and repacking. We have cruised the Alaska coast, the Caribbean, Australia and New Zealand, and the Panama Canal and up the west coast of Mexico and the United States.

Our favorite cruise was the Alaska coast partly because of the exceptional beauty of the area but also because of the company of our great friends Bill & Jo Lewis. We toured, played bridge, had too many cocktails, ate too much food and then did it all over again the next day. Sitting on our outdoor deck sipping black Russians under the midnight sun watching whales pass by is something I will never forget.

Chapter XXIX

Friends

Throughout life one makes many acquaintances. Lots of them rise to the status of friends. In all of our relationships there are friends and then there are FRIENDS. The term best friend is often used but it is very exclusive and implies only one friend can rise to that status. A better term evades me.

As we moved around the country we built friendships in each community in which we lived. Once we moved on relationships were maintained for short times by letters or phone calls and then by a marathon of Christmas cards, each of us not wanting to be the one who ends the relationship. Rarely does a bond of friendship survive long term.

Even more rarely do two couples build a bond of friendship wherein both the males and females share equal closeness. What a special relationship that is. We have been fortunate to have enjoyed two of those close relationships.

Becoming "best friends" is determined by many things. Having common values is one cornerstone. Without respect for each other two people can never be totally close. Having common interests is another cornerstone. Common interests stimulate discussion topics and shared experiences. Trust is a third cornerstone. With a real friend one knows that he or she will be there for you when you need them. They will never let you down. And the fourth cornerstone is a common sense of humor. Being able to laugh together is very important to any relationship. Being able to laugh at one self or at each other is a bonding experience. How often we look back fondly at humorous things that happened with close friends and are reminded of their importance to us.

For nearly forty years Bill and Jo Lewis have been our best friends. At first he was my boss and mentor. Gradually we evolved to a lasting friendship. We have helped each other through a variety of challenges and have always been there for each other.

Bill taught me leadership and empathy for employees. He stood by me in some difficult business times. Conversely, when he had business problems I stood by him. I recall a telephone call from Bill when his drug store business was in trouble wanting to sell me half of a drug store for $50,000. Of course I sent him the money. He insisted on a contract to protect me to which my response was "I don't need a contract, if you can afford to pay me back you will, I can afford to lose the money but I can't afford to lose the friendship". We shared business, golf, drinks, bridge, yard projects, you name it and we did it together.

Jo and Carolyn also bonded. From our first years at Medinah Country Club when our wives, along with our children, would meet us at the pool after golf, to years later when we shared grandchildren and had retirement homes near each other. I recall one evening in Acapulco when we all had been to dinner at a fine restaurant and were appropriately dressed in our better clothes. Back at the house for black Russians Carolyn was crossing a small waterfall by the pool bar and fell in the water. Jo seeing her embarrassment immediately jumped into the pool, also fully dressed. We all followed. That is friendship.

When Carolyn first became ill with MS we bought a home near Bill and Jo in Three Rivers, Michigan. When we visited on weekends or if Carolyn stayed there on her own, Bill and Jo looked after our home and after Carolyn.

We see Bill and Jo less frequently today because of the distance between our homes. The friendship however lives on.

We have also been fortunate to have had a long term, roughly thirty years, relationship with John and Nancy Robb. They lived near us in Butler, Pennsylvania where we shared golf and bridge and a lot of socializing. They now live within miles of us in Naples, Florida and our friendship continues. Our girls were friends as they grew up which gave us common interests and sometimes challenges. It has been a pleasure to see all of the girls grow so well into parenthood.

Chapter XXX

Family

From the time I was a child I heard "family first" or "blood is thicker than water". This philosophy is generally true with all families throughout the world. For some reason there is a normal tendency to watch over and protect members of your own family first. One might recognize shortcomings in a family member but those flaws are generally shelved or stored away for internal use only. All families are cheerleaders for their own members.

Without dwelling on individuals I want to record a few thoughts about some of our family members.

My Grandmother Mary Kirk Pentz (1891 – 1973 est.) : Uneducated, smart, four foot ten at her tallest, and tough as nails. She kept the family together. Always with a calm smile and a warm hug she made us boys love her. I recall my brother and me throwing snowballs down by the local stores when a drunk came out of a bar and said something to us. Grandma told him to get back inside or she would knock him bowlegged.

When she was elderly and walked with a cane some bad elements who had moved into her neighborhood would kick her cane out from under her and rob her. It didn't scare her. She just stayed there and kept fighting.

My Grandfather Clarence Pentz (1885 – 1960): Although illiterate, he worked hard and was able to earn good money as an iron worker. He loved to travel and would do so at the drop of a hat without notice to anyone. Eventually he would reappear and start earning money again. He had high standards of morality and never drank alcohol. He was very prejudiced against the Irish and the Blacks. Most likely this came from competition for the construction jobs. He was buried on St. Patrick's Day and the funeral was attended by a lot of black neighbors. Dad commented that grandpa would roll over in his grave if he knew.

My Grandmother Josephine Miller Meeker (1881 – 1963): An exceptionally smart woman. She was a teacher in her early years and later a housewife. She was a whiz at crossword puzzles, had a great laugh and sense of humor and was a great cook. I recall that she made home made donuts frequently with a large caldron of lard. Pen and I could only watch through the kitchen door for fear of the boiling grease. The wait was well worth it. She was also great with the local birds and squirrels always feeding them.

My Grandfather Clarence Meeker (1882 – 1981): A 1907 graduate of Albany Law School he was an attorney which was a highly respected profession in those days. At one point he was Secretary of Labor for the State of New York under the Republican administration. He could read books faster than anyone I have ever known.

If we gave him a book for Christmas he had it read by the afternoon. He was a mentor to my father.

Having grown up in the country he was a skilled fisherman, hunter, and woodsman. He knew volumes about plants and gardening. He was also a skilled writer and somewhat of an artist, often coloring flowers in the borders of his own stationary. He was a man of honor and integrity. He was a roll model for all of us.

In his later years he spent his time researching and writing a book about the relationship of religion to wars throughout history. He makes many observations about biblical beliefs and their origin. Although he died before his book was published I later retyped it and published it for him.

My Mother, Josephine Meeker Pentz (1912 -): Very smart and very competitive. She was an avid golfer, bowler, bridge player, gardener, painter, knitter and mother. She didn't get much opportunity to opine because she was always surrounded by three type "A" men. She is loved by everyone who knows her and at 97 is still playing bridge. I recall when she was about 89 playing in the Turtle Creek Country Club golf championship for her flight. It was a hot day and she was behind three holes with four to go. Dad was concerned about the heat and said to her why don't you stop because the match is essentially over anyway. That got her competitive goat and she won the next four holes to win the championship. She was also very accomplished in bridge with many master's points. She is a lady.

My Father, Robert "Bob" Pentz (1912 – 2005): His was truly the American success story. From a poorly educated family to having to work at age thirteen to Chairman of the Board for a good sized company he did what it took to succeed. He may have cut corners on occasion but he did what he knew how to do and what he had been taught to do by his mentors.

Incredibly competitive he was an avid golfer, fisherman and gin rummy player. He achieved six hole-in-ones and the club gin rummy championship many times. I recall at age 89 him playing with me in a family scramble event at Quail West. On the eleventh hole, a par three, we had a ball about fifteen feet from the pin. He said "you guys can handle this, I'm tired and I'll wait in the cart." All three of us missed and called him to come over and putt. He sank that putt and we won the tournament.

He was a scrapper. Even in his late eighties he challenged men to step outside. He never really got into fist fights but he talked big. One time when he was about 85 I was with him at his club when he had a disagreement with someone. He said "let's go outside and I'll knock your block off and bring your stupid son with you and my son will kick his ass too." Of course nothing happened.

Dad loved children. As he aged he began stopping at any table in any restaurant where there was a child. He always wanted to thumb wrestle with them and to let them win. He died of Alzheimer's disease at age 93. He was a deservedly proud man and I too am proud of him.

My brother, Robert "Pen" Pentz (1935 – 1990): As covered earlier, the ultimate salesman, intelligent, gregarious and aggressive. Highly skilled in anything he seriously attempted. Pen died at the age of 54 from hepatitis C.

My wife, Carolyn Koontz Pentz (1937 -): Loved by everyone, Carolyn never had an unkind word about anyone. Under the stress of her ailment she maintains a positive attitude and struggles without complaint to do her part. Confined to a wheelchair she makes the best of life.

Spending her entire childhood in one town in the religious south she is naturally conservative. Some hold her on a pedestal. I recall at a three table bridge evening out of frustration over some mistake she said "shit" and everyone stood and applauded.

As a corporate wife she was a great balance and compliment to me. She got along with everyone, did not interfere, gave me her opinions, which were generally more conservative than mine, and she supported me during my most stressful times.

Her greatest asset is motherhood. She stands by her children through thick and thin never being critical of decisions they may make. And they stand by her as well they should.

Our children, Debbie (1959 -), Karen (1965 -), Laurie (1967 -): **Pride** is the best word to describe what our daughters have given to us. They have charged into adulthood with the warmth and gregarious nature of their mother and the get it done persistence of their father. They are loving and caring parents who are dedicated to the care and proper upbringing of their children. They are organized and tireless in their work pursuits. They are the assurance of our own eternal life. They are our daughters.

Our grandchildren: What a joy it is to see the grandchildren do well as they too grow toward adulthood. I thought I was pretty good in the sporting arena – they are better. I was a good student – they are better. I thought I was empathetic – they are better. I recall when I was a child our family doctor told my mother that every child should exceed their parents in size and capability. Our grandchildren are proving him to have been correct.

As I look back at what I have recorded here, it occurs to me that in a short span of about 125 years, from the birth of my grandfather to now, the world has changed beyond belief. Consider that when my grandfather was a child there were no light bulbs, no cars, no airplanes, no radio or television or telephone, no power tools, no antibiotics and no computers. Houses were heated with coal or wood, cooking was done with wood stoves, refrigeration was dependent upon ice that was cut from the frozen lakes in the winter and stored in sawdust to keep it insulated through the summer. How far we have come.

In the early 1900s someone proposed that the government patent office should be closed because everything had already been invented. I recall my teacher in high school reading us an old article wherein an opponent of automobiles opined that at speeds exceeding forty miles per hour people's hearts and eyes would burst from the pressure. Today our space travelers exceed 20,000 miles per hour.

We have gone from the time when the grocer wrote the prices of your purchase on the side of the brown paper bag and then added the total before packaging the items in the same bag, to cash registers, to computers, to the bar code, to automatic inventory controls.

I recall my college days when everyone had a holster with a slide rule hanging from his belt. Our grandchildren will probably never see a slide rule as they now have enormous computer power in the palms of their hands.

And medicine has changed with the development of antibiotics and vaccines to organ transplants and now to the charting of the human genome. Will this lead to the production of replacement parts and to the prevention of diseases by anticipating their arrival and initiating treatment in advance? Without a doubt it will.

We have put men on the moon and are now planning a long term moon station wherein people from earth will live. What will the next hundred years bring about?

Our grandchildren face a different education system from what we knew. There is more to learn and the topics are different from what we were taught. The days of summer vacation so that the kids could help with the crops are coming to an end. We have gone from an agrarian society to an industrial and technical society with science and math replacing farming as our foundation. Our grandchildren will rise to the occasion and they will take it in stride as do all generations. They are the future.

LaVergne, TN USA
01 September 2009
156678LV00001B/19/P